Andrew Webster Archibald

The Bible Verified

Andrew Webster Archibald

The Bible Verified

ISBN/EAN: 9783742809803

Manufactured in Europe, USA, Canada, Australia, Japa

Cover: Foto ©Lupo / pixelio.de

Manufactured and distributed by brebook publishing software (www.brebook.com)

Andrew Webster Archibald

The Bible Verified

THE

BIBLE VERIFIED.

BY THE
REV. ANDREW W. ARCHIBALD.

WITH AN

INTRODUCTORY NOTE

By PROF. RANSOM B. WELCH, D.D., LL.D.,
OF AUBURN THEOLOGICAL SEMINARY.

PHILADELPHIA:
PRESBYTERIAN BOARD OF PUBLICATION
AND SABBATH-SCHOOL WORK,
1334 CHESTNUT STREET.

COPYRIGHT, 1890, BY

THE TRUSTEES OF THE

**PRESBYTERIAN BOARD OF PUBLICATION
AND SABBATH-SCHOOL WORK.**

All Rights Reserved.

WESTCOTT & THOMSON,
Stereotypers and Electrotypers, Philada.

TO HIS CHILDREN,

WARREN, KENNETH AND CECIL,

THIS VOLUME IS AFFECTIONATELY DEDICATED

BY THE AUTHOR.

PREFACE TO SECOND EDITION.

THE Author wishes to express his gratification at the generous reception which has been given to his unambitious literary and religious venture—a reception so cordial that, within six weeks of the issue of the first edition, he is informed of the need of a second. For this he adds, upon the Bible and the Monuments, two chapters, which have aimed at popularizing archæological lore, which have cost him no little labor, but which in their materials have been to him of absorbing and even romantic interest, and which he feels will give completeness to the volume.

A. W. A.

PREFACE.

The following pages were not originally prepared with any thought of publication. They are sermons that have been preached in the ordinary course of a busy pastorate. They were not a set series of discourses even. In these days of biblical criticism questions as to the authority of the Scriptures have arisen from time to time. To answer these inquiries, which have made their way into the popular mind, a sermon would be preached along one line, and in the course of time another along a different line. So doubtful was the author about launching a volume upon the sea of public thought that he concluded to offer for publication what he has written only on the condition of a favorable judgment and of encouragement from two of his former highly-esteemed instructors — Prof. R. B. Welch, D. D., LL.D., formerly of Union College (later of Auburn Theological Seminary), and Prof. G. E. Day, D. D., of the Yale Divinity School and one of the American Old-Testament Committee in the preparation of the Revised Version of the Scriptures.

The author hopes that both clergy and laity may find the book to be stimulating and helpful, and that they may discover no glaring mistakes in statements of fact or in expressions of opinion. Where there is room for different conclusions he has simply stated his own, without a nice balancing of arguments pro and con. which would be unsuitable for the pulpit.

He frankly confesses to leaning toward the conservative side of the issues raised by the Higher Criticism. In the fulfillment of prophecy he cannot speak disparagingly, as one eminent Christian scholar does, of dwelling upon "remarkable minute correspondences between old-time prognostications and new-time events." He is ready to be as old-fashioned as the New-Testament writers, who did see in the minutiæ of history secondary, if not primary, fulfillment of previous predictions. Some examples may be mentioned. Prediction in Zechariah: "Behold, thy King cometh unto thee: . . . lowly, and riding upon an ass, even upon a colt the foal of an ass"; corresponding fact to which John calls attention: "And Jesus, having found a young ass, sat thereon." Prediction in Isaiah: "He opened not his mouth"; fact in Matthew: "And he gave him no answer, not even to one word." Prediction in the Psalms: "In my thirst they gave me vinegar to drink"; fact in Matthew: "One of them ran, and took a sponge, and filled it with vinegar, and put it on a reed, and gave him to drink." Prediction in the Psalms: "They part my garments among them, and upon my vesture do they cast lots"; fact in John: "The soldiers therefore, when they had crucified Jesus, took his garments, and made four parts, to every soldier a part; and also the coat: now the coat was without seam, woven from the top throughout. They said therefore one to another, Let us not rend it, but cast lots for it, whose it shall be." Prediction in Exodus regarding the paschal lamb: "Neither shall ye break a bone thereof"; fact in John regarding the Lamb of God: "When they came to Jesus, they brake not his legs." Prediction in Zechariah: "They shall look unto me whom they have pierced"; fact in John: "Howbeit one of the soldiers with a spear pierced his side." These illustrations—and they might be multiplied—are sufficient to justify not only the tracing of great lines of prophecy, but also the verifying in detail of predictions.

No claim is made to originality. The writer is indebted to the standard authorities along the various lines of his research. Professor Welch has kindly written an Introductory Note, for which the Author is grateful. The writer also desires to say how he has been reassured in a sometimes wavering purpose by private letters (quoted by permission) from Professor Day, who in the reading of the manuscript was "increasingly interested" as he proceeded, who bore testimony to the "fresh and popular treatment given to the interesting subjects discussed," and who recognized in the discourses "grasp of thought and fullness of illustration and balance of judgment."

The Author would simply add that the volume includes two sermons written after he had submitted his manuscript to his scholarly critics, and, not wishing to trouble them further, he ventures to insert without their critical supervision the discourses on "Formidable Objections to the Bible" and "Biblical Signs preceding the Destruction of Jerusalem."

A. W. A.

INTRODUCTORY NOTE.

By Professor RANSOM B. WELCH.

It gives me pleasure to say that when a professor in college I knew the author of these sermons as a student. He was diligent, accurate, trustworthy; waiting ever to report until he had found; then reporting unostentatiously, but truthfully and sympathetically, what he had found.

This gave assurance that if he ever ventured into authorship he would be an honest writer, aiming to furnish real information, striving earnestly to convince others because of his own thorough conviction, patiently guiding and lovingly helping others because he himself by patience and hope had sought and found.

His is a judicial rather than a partisan spirit, loyal to the truth, yet liberal toward honest doubt and sincere search—the more tolerant because the more truthful.

The general subject of the book is important. The particular topics are timely. The treatment is vigorous and truthful. The style is clear, compact and in keeping with the plan and purpose of the sermons. The book is never dull, while it is always instructive, and at times especially impressive and quickening. It mainly pursues the historic method, which, if not the exclusive, is the most ready and effective, method for such a course of sermons. The author does not claim to be original, but wisely avails himself of facts both recent and remote in almost every field of investigation. These facts are not only informing, but they serve also the twofold purpose of argumentation and illustration, stimulating the attention while they convince the judgment.

The book cannot fail to reflect credit upon the author and light upon the reader.

We heartily commend it to all who would the better understand some of the vital questions of these stirring times—who would search the Scriptures, especially to seek and find the truth as it is in Jesus.

RANSOM B. WELCH.

AUBURN THEO. SEMINARY.

CONTENTS.

	PAGE
INTRODUCTORY NOTE, By Prof. R. B. Welch	9

CHAPTER I.
The Canon; or, What Constitutes the Bible? . . . 13

CHAPTER II.
The Bible in Manuscript 25

CHAPTER III.
The Bible in English 39

CHAPTER IV.
The Inspiration of the Bible 52

CHAPTER V.
The Bible and the Miraculous 65

CHAPTER VI.
Formidable Objections to the Bible 79

CHAPTER VII.
Incidental Confirmations of the Bible 91

CONTENTS.

CHAPTER VIII.
                                                              PAGE
THE BIBLE AND SCIENCE; OR, THE CREATIVE WEEK . 108

CHAPTER IX.
THE BIBLE AND THE MUMMIES OF THE PHARAOHS . 121

CHAPTER X.
ELEVATING INFLUENCE OF THE BIBLE 136

CHAPTER XI.
THE BIBLE AND THE GOLDEN CITY OF BABYLON . . 151

CHAPTER XII.
THE BIBLE AND THE COMMERCIAL CITY OF TYRE . . 164

CHAPTER XIII.
BIBLICAL SIGNS PRECEDING THE DESTRUCTION OF JE-
    RUSALEM 179

CHAPTER XIV.
THE BIBLE AND THE DESTRUCTION OF JERUSALEM . . 190

CHAPTER XV.
THE BIBLE AND THE PECULIAR JEWS 202

CHAPTER XVI.
THE BIBLE AND THE MONUMENTS—EGYPT AND ASSYRIA. 216

CHAPTER XVII.
THE BIBLE AND THE MONUMENTS—BABYLONIA AND
    PALESTINE. 236

THE BIBLE VERIFIED.

CHAPTER I.

THE CANON; OR, WHAT CONSTITUTES THE BIBLE?

"Ye search the Scriptures, because ye think that in them ye have eternal life; and these are they which bear witness of Me."—JOHN 5 : 39.

A VERY natural inquiry in these days, when we are searching for the foundations of things, is, What exactly is the Bible? What books constitute the Scriptures? "These are they," says our text, indicating a definite number.

1. The reference, of course, is simply to the Old Testament, and the contents of this have been fixed for ages with tolerable certainty. While the books from Genesis to Malachi were composed at different points of a period covering more than a thousand years, they seem to have been gathered into one sacred collection some four hundred years before the Christian era. They were arranged under three great divisions, which Christ once called the Law, the Prophets, and the Psalms. This meant

something specific, for we find the same threefold division used by the son of Sirach at least 130 B. C., and by Philo, who was born only a few years before Christ, and by Josephus, who was born 37 A. D. It was as if different persons to-day should refer to the three volumes of Motley's *Dutch Republic*. It would prove that such a work existed and in that form. Both Philo and Josephus quote from each of the three great divisions and from most of the individual books, giving us the same evidence for the genuineness of the Old Testament as we would have for Motley's *Dutch Republic* if different authors should quote from each volume and from nearly every separate chapter.

Josephus even gives the precise number of books comprised in the whole—"only twenty two," he says. But that contradicts the number at present received, does it not? We count thirty-nine. The variation is easily explained. Originally there was not the arbitrary division into First and Second of Chronicles, First and Second of Kings, First and Second of Samuel. These double books were each considered one, as they properly are. In like manner, the Lamentations of Jeremiah were joined to his prophecy, Ruth was attached to Judges (of which it is a continuation), Ezra and Nehemiah were reckoned as one because they treated of the same period, and the twelve Minor Prophets naturally fell into one class. With a grouping of this kind we can easily get the "only twenty-two books" in the Old Testament, and Josephus was particular about having it twenty-two, that it might conform to the number of letters in the Hebrew alphabet. When, then, the text speaks of the Scriptures as "these are they," it refers to exactly the same books, according to these ancient witnesses, as are now in our possession.

Again, all down the ages of the Christian era our present books are frequently named, giving us a continuous line of testimony. It should also be remembered that the Old-Testament Scriptures for nineteen centuries have been held in sacred trust by two great religious parties of antagonistic beliefs, the Jews and Christians. It is as though, to use the illustration of another, they were guarding "the same casket of jewels," and a single gem could not have been removed without detection by the other. It is the strongest kind of evidence, when opposing parties thus agree, that each has been honest in neither adding to nor subtracting from the holy oracles, for the Hebrew Bible of the Jew is the Old Testament of the Christian.

But how about the Apocrypha? The Roman Catholics, you are aware, at the Council of Trent in 1546 formally adopted it as a part of the Bible. But Josephus expressly says that it was not "of the like authority" with the Scriptures, and Philo does not refer to it authoritatively as he does to the Old Testament, and it is not endorsed by New-Testament references, as the recognized Jewish

Canon was, except that Jude endorses a sentiment from the apocryphal book of Enoch, much as Paul adopted a sentiment of a Greek poet in the sermon to the Athenians. How, then, did the Apocrypha ever become associated with the Old Testament? The explanation is, that the Jews of Alexandria had the Scriptures translated into Greek, which they spoke in Egypt. To this Greek or Septuagint version (which was begun about 280 B. C.) other Jewish books, written after the prophetic age, were added from time to time for convenient use ecclesiastically or because of laxer views entertained in Egypt than in Palestine. Now, since Greek came into wider use than any other language, this Greek translation, with its Apocrypha attached to the Old-Testament Scriptures, became the Bible with which most people were familiar, and by degrees the distinction between the Old Testament and Apocrypha became effaced. Thus all down the centuries there have been individuals who have reckoned the Apocrypha as inspired, and the Council of Trent finally committed the Papal Church to that position. Even Protestants long had a lingering feeling of reverence for the Apocrypha, and hence bound it in with the Scriptures, where it should not be, because it is not recognized as Scripture by Josephus, Philo, or the New-Testament writers. When Christ said, "These are they," he referred to the Old Testament alone as existing in the threefold division of the Law, the Prophets, and the Psalms.

2. While we are thus clear as to the contents of the Old Testament, we may not be so sure as to what constitutes the New, for the great Teacher never pointed out the New-Testament books, since they were not written till after his death. So far as the Old Testament was concerned, he only endorsed what the general religious consensus had decided beforehand. The limits of the Old Testament were fixed at least two or three centuries before he was born, and that not by any miraculous interposition, but by a providential agreement among the most pious and enlightened as to what was inspired. That is the way in which the proper contents of the New Testament have been determined. It was a matter of growth through devout criticism. Some thought such a book was inspired, and some another; some that this one ought to be rejected, and some that that one ought to be; and so arguments were balanced until there was a general agreement among the vast majority of Christians, the exceptions being rare. That is how we got our New Testament. It was not let down in a body from heaven, it was not compiled by the apostles. No divine hand selected its different books with the utterance, "These are they." The inspired Gospels and Epistles did not come to us as magical formularies, but as writings historically belonging to the apostolic age. There is nothing mysterious or mythical in their origin; they come to us as history.

Glancing at the first few centuries of the Christian era, we can see how the New Testament was formed—not suddenly and miraculously, but gradually and naturally. We see it quoted again and again by writers of the second and third centuries. Here is Clement of Rome, for instance, at the end of the first century even (95 A. D.), using expressions found in Hebrews, and in writing to the Corinthians he says: "Take up the Epistle of the blessed Paul the apostle; what was it that he first wrote to you . . . ?" Clement quotes from or alludes to sixteen of the New-Testament books. Ignatius, who suffered martyrdom not far from 107 A. D., in addressing the Ephesians speaks of a "letter" to them by "St. Paul, the sanctified and martyred," and he has repeated references to various New-Testament books. Polycarp, who was burned at the stake 155 or 167 A. D., and who, says Irenæus, a disciple of his, had often talked "with the apostle John and with the rest who had seen the Lord,"— Polycarp tells the Philippians to "look diligently" into what had been written them by the "blessed and glorious Paul;" and he shows a knowledge of three of the Gospels and at least of thirteen of the Epistles. The three, Clement, Ignatius, and Polycarp, refer to all of the New-Testament books except Second and Third John and Jude.

Justin Martyr, who wrote about 150 A. D., speaks of a "revelation which was made" to John, and he refers either directly or indirectly to nearly every

New-Testament book. Irenæus, who flourished from 130 to 200 A. D., uses this language: "Peter says in his Epistle"; also, "Paul, when writing to the Romans"; and he quotes from or alludes to every book in the New Testament except Philemon and Third John, and there are only fifty-four chapters to which he has no reference. Tertullian (born about 150 A. D.) quotes from all of the New-Testament books except four, and possibly two. Clement of Alexandria (160 to 220 A. D.) seems to allude to all except two. Origen (born about 186 A. D.) has citations embracing, it is asserted by Tregelles, two-thirds of the entire New Testament. It is even claimed that an English lord has found in the writings of the first three centuries the whole New Testament with the exception of eleven verses. To such an extent have the apostolic writings been woven into the earliest literature of our era that their genuineness cannot be doubted. They are a part of history.

While they can thus be clearly traced back to the beginning, there was more or less confusion at first as to their divine authority. The line was not at once sharply drawn separating them from other writings and making them pre-eminently sacred. Irenæus, for example, quoted as "Scripture" the "Shepherd" of Hermas, who probably wrote it a little before the middle of the second century. Clement of Alexandria also considered it "divine" or inspired, as he did the Epistle of the Roman

Clement (95 A. D.), and as he did that of Barnabas, whose date is not later than 125 A. D. These writings are close to the apostolic age, and they were not infrequently read in the churches as Scripture. They have come down to us, and are very interesting, but are uninspired, as we think. Their inspiration was also denied by many from the outset. An ancient catalogue (the Muratorian Fragment, 150 to 170 A. D.), while including all of the New Testament except First and Second of Peter, James and Hebrews, rejects the "Shepherd," because of its having been composed "recently, in our own times, by Hermas, while his brother Pius was bishop of the see of Rome." In the course of time it was universally rejected as uncanonical, as also were the Epistles of Clement and Barnabas. The same fate awaited a work called the "Apocalypse of Peter," which at one time was received in some quarters.

In other words, here were writings (and there were still others) which many used to consider Scripture, but which eventually were dropped out of the list of sacred books. There was no formal vote taken on their rejection, but they gradually came to be regarded by the Church at large as of inferior rank. There was a sifting process going on. Here would be a letter claiming to be Paul's, there another claiming to be Peter's. What was the truth? Each case was discussed, not in an ecclesiastical council, but by the general Church.

Some would take the affirmative, and some the negative, and thus one book after another was considered on its merits, and in this way the canon was formed. It took several centuries to come with anything like unanimity to the result which is now almost universally accepted as correct. This is what might have been expected. Away in the East would be an apostolic letter which the people of the West would know nothing about for fifty or a hundred years, and therefore results were reached slowly. It was a question as to whether several of the present New-Testament books should be admitted—a question raised not by infidels, but by Christians.

The witnesses were perfectly frank and honest. Origen testifies that Peter left one Epistle, "and perhaps a second, for that is disputed." He also says, "John wrote the Apocalypse (Revelation) and an Epistle of very few lines; and it may be a second and a third, since all do not admit them to be genuine." In quoting from James and Jude he adds that their canonicity was doubted. Eusebius (born about 270 A. D.) gives in his church history a list of the New-Testament books. He classes the great majority as among the "universally acknowledged." As acknowledged "by the most" he names Jude, James, Second Peter, Second and Third John. Revelation, he says, "some reject, while others reckon it among the books acknowledged," although in his opinion it would be received by all in "due" time. The candid weighing of evidence continued, until Athanasius (365 A. D.), in naming the contents of the canon, gave the exact books which we have, and only those. Eusebius and Athanasius were as near to the apostles as we are to the Landing of the Pilgrims. Jerome, who died 420 A. D., adopted the same list that we now have.

Councils about this time "sanctioned and ratified," as another has said, "what had already taken place spontaneously" and by a "steady growth." Thus have the limits of our New Testament been fixed by the general Christian consciousness guided by historical data. No council decided the matter, no heavenly voice did, but the result has been reached by patient comparing of views. There is not perfect unanimity yet on the part of the Christian world. Now and then a devout scholar at present doubts the canonical authority of the Second and Third of John or the Second of Peter; but even if these were rejected the system of Christianity would not be affected, any more than would the facts of our Civil War be disproved if it should turn out that some historian did not write certain two or three chapters of the work bearing his name. Still, the almost universal sentiment accepts all the books of the present New Testament, so that we can say of them, as Christ said of the Old-Testament books, "These are they," confident that they constitute the true word of God.

THE CANON.

Our Bible comes to us not by magic or witchery of any kind, but through historical channels, and if some new apostolic writing were discovered it could properly be admitted into the canon, not because of some miraculous endorsement from the sky, but on historical grounds; and it seems to be historically probable that inspired Epistles have been lost. Paul, for instance, in 1 Cor. 5 : 9 says: "I wrote unto you in my Epistle," thus alluding to a letter previously written to the Corinthians, but this is not now extant. And in Col. 4 : 16 he says, "When this Epistle has been read among you, cause that it be read also in the church of the Laodiceans; and that ye also read the Epistle from Laodicea;" but we have no letter to the Laodiceans, unless the Epistle to the Ephesians was, as some think, a circular letter designed also for the Laodiceans. Now, if these two lost Epistles of the apostle to which he refers should ever be unearthed, they would go through the same course of criticism as our present New-Testament books went through, and if the wellnigh universal opinion should in the end be favorable to their authenticity, they could consistently be placed with Paul's other letters. That is, our Bible has not a mythical, but an historical, basis, and it stands all the stronger before the world for that reason.

We do not worship ignorantly; ours is not a blind superstition; we believe on evidence. We challenge attention to the origin of our sacred books. They were not produced, to use a Pauline expression, "in a corner." They have been open to all from the beginning, so that whosoever would might read. Let us be grateful to a kind Providence which has so worked them into the very warp and woof of history that their credibility cannot be attacked without taking issue with the great fact of human development itself. Our faith is founded on the clear word of God, and there we rest as on a rock, upon which the tide of infidelity has been beating in vain for all the centuries that are past. The waves of skeptical assault have broken upon it only to be dissipated into spray and foam. The grand old Bible seems to lift itself in triumph after each shock, exactly as the rock appears to emerge from the breakers when the ocean tide has spent its force.[1]

CHAPTER II.

THE BIBLE IN MANUSCRIPT.

"The cloak that I left at Troas with Carpus, bring when thou comest, and the books, especially the parchments."— 2 TIM. 4:13.

THIS was a message sent by Paul from his prison at Rome to Timothy, whom the apostle desired to come and see him, and not to forget to fetch the books, and especially the parchments, left behind with a friend at Troas. We do not know what important works these were. They may have contained some of his own inspired Epistles, and very likely portions at least of the Old-Testament Scriptures, for he was a man who read his Bible. The sacred writings were to him very precious. Perhaps he had been hurried off to the Roman imprisonment without being permitted to take his books, among which, we may be sure, would be the Holy Scriptures.

He could not send out and get a copy of the Bible for a trifling amount, as we can now. When a work is rare it is expensive. For instance, one of the very first printed books was the Latin Bible in 1546, and a copy of this edition not long ago sold in New York for eight thousand dollars, while an English earl paid for a copy over sixteen thousand dollars. The rarity of the work is what constitutes its value, and in the apostolic age, before the days of printing, books were rare, as they are not now, when with stereotype plates they can be produced with ease, rapidity and economy. There was then no such thing as a press to run off large editions. If a second copy was wanted, it had to be laboriously written out by hand.

There were those who made this copying a distinct business. Paul had an amanuensis, for in Rom. 16 : 22 we read, 'I, Tertius, who wrote the Epistle, salute you." The apostle only added a postscript in his own familiar chirography, as we learn from 1 Cor. 16 : 21 : "The salutation of me Paul with mine own hand."

The writing was done upon two kinds of material. From the reeds which grew along the Nile was manufactured an article called papyrus, resembling, yet different from, our paper. Then the skins of young antelopes and other animals were dressed into a fine sort of vellum, which was more durable, and as a consequence more costly, than the former. When Paul sent for "the books, especially the parchments," it was literally for the papyrus rolls and the vellum rolls, and the latter particularly he wanted because they were worth more.

But he did not wish either of them to be lost. He perhaps was afraid they might be carelessly thrown aside and destroyed. If they contained any of his Epistles, the fate of these he would naturally fear. He might have heard the story of Aristotle's priceless works long lying unknown in a cellar, where, fortunately, after two centuries, they were discovered. The apostle's fears were justified, as we of modern times can see better than he did. How much of literature has been nearly lost, being only providentially—or, as we say, accidentally—recovered! The great work of Quintilian was brought to light in the fifteenth century from a dark and filthy dungeon. There have been the most romantic discoveries of this kind. A copy of Propertius, the Latin poet, was found stained and crumpled under the casks of a wine-cellar. Three hundred lines of Homer's Odyssey were taken from the hands of a mummy. The original manuscript of Magna Charta, that great charter of English liberty and constitutional freedom in general, was saved at the critical moment when a tailor was about to cut it into patterns. In 1626 a German in excavating for a new house on the site of an old one came upon a well-wrapped parcel, which proved to be Luther's *Table Talk*, the only copy in existence, and a most valuable work because of the vivid picture which it gives of the Reformer's life and times.

These discoveries have been odd enough, but there is a still stranger way in which literary treasures once lost have been found. The vellum, the parchment, mentioned in the text, which was prepared from skins, was so very costly that it was frequently cleansed and used again after the manner of a slate. The vegetable ink was as nearly obliterated as possible, but in the course of time the old characters have reappeared, very indistinct and yet visible. Once in a while the vellum has been cleaned a second time, and a third writing has been committed to its face. In either case great skill is required to decipher the first characters. Still, it has been done, and behold, a long-lost work of Cicero and other classics have thus been given to the world! Providence has in this way cared for the Bible.

In the National Library at Paris there long lay an ancient document containing sermons and other compositions of Ephraem of Syria, a Church Father of the fourth century. The preservation of his writings was fortunate, but underneath these were at last discovered traces of another text. This was in the latter half of the seventeenth century. Various attempts were made to decipher the old and obscured characters, but without success till about fifty years ago, when by chemical appliances the hidden text was made out and published. It proved to be a manuscript of the larger portion of the New Testament, dating back to the fifth century. In the twelfth century some copyist had taken the leaves apart, erased the old text, and written in its place the works of Ephraem, while the whole was bound together anew. In the new volume formed the leaves were all disarranged, and many of them were upside down, so far as the first writing was concerned. This made the decipherment all the more difficult to the scholar who undertook the confusing task; who, however, succeeded, and the result is one of the best manuscript authorities we have in biblical criticism. Who could have ever imagined that a writing of the fifth century would thus be made to reveal its secrets to the nineteenth century? Well may we exclaim, What hath God wrought! He has evidently had all the solicitude that Paul had for valuable parchments. When we realize that many precious manuscripts have been lost, we can appreciate the apostle's anxiety for those books and parchments at Troas.

None of the original manuscripts of the Bible have been preserved. Shall we therefore reject this book? As well might we throw away the works of Homer, who flourished from eight to nine hundred years before Christ, but of whose writings we have no complete copy older than the thirteenth century, and no fragments even older than the sixth century—fifteen centuries after the blind poet died. Of the history by Herodotus there is no manuscript extant earlier than the ninth century, but this historian lived in the fifth century before the Christian era. There is no copy of Plato previous to the ninth century, and he wrote considerably more than a thousand years before that. Less than three hundred years intervene between the oldest Bible manuscripts and the apostolic age. What if we do not have the original manuscripts of the inspired volume? Must we read every author in his own handwriting? Do we have Hume and Gibbon and Bancroft and Motley in manuscript in our libraries? No, but we have no doubt of possessing their works. It is a matter of history that they have lived and that they wrote the books going under their respective names. So are we sure of the genuineness of the sacred books. We have none of the original manuscripts, but all through the second and third and successive centuries the New and Old Testaments are quoted, and therefore must have been in existence. And so far as manuscripts are concerned, we have older ones of the Scriptures than of any uninspired writings.

The method of determining their age might here be briefly indicated. The Bible has at different times been differently divided, not always into our present chapters and verses. About 340 A. D. divisions of a certain order were introduced (a system perfected by Eusebius), and about 460 A. D. divisions of another order (the stichometrical) became prevalent. Now, of course, if a manuscript contains the Eusebian divisions the date must be after 340 A. D.; if the stichometrical, after 460 A. D. If an old Bible should come into your hands without any date, the question would be, When was it printed? A friend suggests that it must have been issued from the press as early as 1500 A. D., but you say no, and you call attention to the present verse division. Well, what of it? Nothing, only that that fact shows the printing to have been after the year 1551, when this verse arrangement was first made. In ways like this the age of manuscripts is learned with great precision, and thus has it been proved that, though we do not have the original manuscripts of the Bible, we do have parchments of very great antiquity. How grateful we should be to God who has so wonderfully guarded them through the ages, thus giving us stronger testimony for the authenticity of the Scriptures than for that of the ancient classics! Our faith should be strengthened by evidence so conclusive, and our affections ought to cluster around the parchments as tenaciously as did Paul's. Three of these manuscripts, because of their great age, deserve special notice.

1. The Alexandrian Manuscript is assigned to the fifth century. The translators who gave us the King James version of the Scriptures did not have access to it, for they finished their work in 1611, whereas 1628 was the year when this manuscript was donated to Charles the First of England by the patriarch of Constantinople, who got it in Egypt at Alexandria, and hence the name, Alexandrian Manuscript. It is now in the British Museum, so fragile that it is kept under glass and the use of it is confined to scholars, who have access to

it for textual purposes. The vellum is somewhat decayed, there being holes in it, and some of the letters are worn away along the margin. Whole leaves are missing. More than twenty-four chapters of Matthew have at some time dropped out, and there are other omissions. It, however, contains most of the Old and New Testaments, besides other writings, including the only genuine Epistle of Clement to the Corinthians—that Clement who died about the year 100, and who is supposed to be the one mentioned by Paul in Philippians (4 : 3) as a fellow-worker.

2. Of still higher value is the Vatican Manuscript, in the Papal Library at Rome. The first trace we get of it is in the year 1475, when it appears in a catalogue, the earliest made of the library. When Napoleon was at the zenith of his power it was transferred to Paris, but in 1815 came Waterloo, and the manuscript was returned to Rome, where ever since it has been jealously guarded, especially from Protestant inspection. The great English critic Tregelles, with a commendatory letter from a cardinal, went in 1845 to examine it, but he was closely watched by two prelates, who took the precaution to search his pockets and to remove therefrom pen, paper and ink, and if he was noticed giving particular attention to any passage, the volume was snatched from his hands. He only succeeded in making, unobserved, some notes upon his cuffs and finger-

nails. In 1866, Tischendorf, the eminent German scholar, was more successful, giving the world a complete copy. While it lacks a large part of Genesis, thirty of the Psalms, Titus, Timothy, Revelation and still other parts, it comprises the bulk of the Old and New Testaments. It belongs to the fourth century, and is thus a hundred years earlier than the Alexandrian. It may be one of the fifty copies of the Greek Scriptures which the emperor Constantine ordered to be prepared about 331 A. D., and which, when finished, were conveyed to him, says our authority, "in one of the government wagons" for the imperial inspection. Whether it be one of those copies or not, it, at any rate, according to the best critics, dates back to 300 or 350 A. D.[2]

3. To the same century, the fourth, belongs another manuscript, the narrative of whose discovery a few years ago, not at Troas, but at Sinai, reads like a romance. The hero is Tischendorf, whose first name (Lobegott) means in German "Praise God"—a name given him out of gratitude, we are told, because "a strange fear of the mother that her babe would be born blind had not come true." And he was by no means born blind. No man ever had keener sight, and he spent his life in deciphering old manuscripts which other eyes could not read. He believed there were many of these "hidden in dust and darkness."

He started on a tour of investigation, and in

May, 1844, he was in the vicinity of Sinai, where the Law was given through Moses, and where at this time was a group of antique buildings called the Convent of St. Catharine. For many centuries it had been the home of a brotherhood of monks. A rich library had grown up in the distant past, but the spirit of learning had long since died out. The convent was now occupied by twenty or thirty ignorant hermits, who practiced their monastic rites and entertained travelers as occasion offered. It was a peculiar haunt or retreat, being enclosed by a wall forty feet in height. The place of entrance was thirty feet high, and to this aperture or door in the wall the visitor had to be elevated "by a rope." Up this rope Tischendorf first sent his credentials, and, these being satisfactory, he himself was hauled up.

He had access to the library, and while examining the volumes on the shelves he noticed a basket of waste material on the floor awaiting use as kindling, two basketfuls of similar fragments having already served that purpose. Picking over the musty pieces, he came upon several leaves of the Old Testament in Greek, evidently very ancient. He was allowed to take forty-three of these leaves, but the rest of the manuscript had assumed a new value now that the learned stranger seemed anxious for its possession. He departed, telling the monks to take good care of what remained, and he returned home, depositing the forty-three leaves in the University Library at Leipzig.

Some years passed away, but he did not forget the treasure left behind at Sinai. He tried twice— once through a friend and again in person—to secure the parchment or at least a copy of the manuscript, but he failed. With credentials from the Czar of Russia, the head of the Greek Church, he was once more in the Sinaitic convent in the year 1859, but the long-desired treasure was nowhere to be seen, and he was about to leave disappointed when one afternoon he and the steward of the convent walked out together, coming back about sundown. The conversation had been about books, and the steward, inviting him into his cell for supper, brought from a corner a bulky volume wrapped in red cloth. The scholarly German immediately recognized the book; there were some of the very leaves he had rescued from the waste-basket fifteen years before.

This Sinaitic Manuscript contained most of the Old Testament, the whole of the New, besides the Epistle of Barnabas and the Shepherd of Hermas, the authors of which both flourished before 140 A. D. Tischendorf, concealing his emotions to the best of his ability, asked carelessly if he could take the volume to his room and look it over more leisurely. Once out of sight with it, he "fairly danced for joy." All night long by the dim light of a candle he was engaged in copying. He managed to keep control of it long enough to get a complete copy, and the original itself was finally gotten to St. Petersburg "under the form of a loan," and the loan seems likely to be made perpetual, though not without bitter protest from the owners. Fac-simile copies have been made of it and donated to various great libraries.

Such are the most ancient manuscripts which have appeared in modern times to assist in establishing the word of God. Their preservation has been marvelous, providential and almost miraculous. The last two of them are so old they may have been read by Eusebius when our ancestors were barbarians who could neither read nor write. They put the Scriptures on a surer basis than exists for Homer, Herodotus, Plato, Aristotle, Cicero or any other ancient author.

Still stronger manuscript evidence for the genuineness of the Bible may in the years to come be produced. This is an age of discovery, and valuable works may yet be unearthed, when we recollect that a century and a third ago (1750–60), in the excavations at Pompeii, books buried there in 79 A. D. came forth to startle the world, and when we remember that the Sinaitic Manuscript, a parchment of the fourth century, was found less than thirty years ago. Perhaps some of Paul's Epistles in the handwriting of Tertius, with a postscript by himself, will yet appear. The apostle sent for his "books, especially the parchments," but he may have never received them from Troas; they may be lying buried now somewhere about that city.

where he left them with his friend Carpus. What if Schliemann, in his excavations at Troy or Troas, should find not Homeric relics, but Paul's books and parchments? The future alone can disclose what Troas and other old cities may possess in the way of biblical manuscripts.[3] Meanwhile let us be grateful for the parchments which a kind Providence has already brought down to us from antiquity. We have of the New Testament more than a thousand manuscripts, which prove it beyond a shadow of doubt to be genuine. We should cherish what has thus been divinely kept for our benefit through the ages.

Perhaps we do not have for the Scriptures that intense love which the apostle had. How he longed to have by him his books and parchments! Among these may have been some sacred volume given him, it may be, by an affectionate mother while a boy at Tarsus, or a gift from that married sister at Jerusalem whose son once saved his life from a Jewish mob. He may have carried it all through his eventful career, amid the perils on the sea, amid the perils among the robbers, in hunger and thirst, in cold and nakedness. Everywhere it had been his comfort, fortifying him for every emergency, and now that he was in a Roman dungeon, with the long nights of a dreary winter coming on, and with sure death from the monster Nero in the spring, he seems to have wanted again the old Bible, left with his other books and parchments at Troas. The volume would be doubly interesting from its associations if given him in the long ago, when, as Farrar has beautifully pictured him, "little dreaming of all that would befall him, he played, a happy boy, in the dear old Tarsian home." Have any of us such a treasure, a present to us in childhood, with a loved name written below ours on the fly-leaf? If we have, let us hunt it up, brush away the dust on its covers, and, as we recall the golden past, and as the tears start to our eyes because of tender memories, let us open it and once more read prayerfully its warnings and encouragements. One thing is certain: when we come to face death as Paul did, we shall ask for the old book, and somehow it will be very dear then, not only because it was perhaps a gift of a mother or a sister gone to heaven, but because it will be a message of life from the glorified Saviour himself.

> "How precious is the book divine
> By inspiration given!
> Bright as a lamp its doctrines shine,
> To guide our souls to heaven."

CHAPTER III.

THE BIBLE IN ENGLISH.

"Every man heard them speaking in his own language."—
ACTS 2: 6.

THE Old Testament, as all are aware, was written in Hebrew,[1] and the New in Greek. But the divine plan has been to communicate the truth to each nationality in its own tongue. At Pentecost there were representatives from "every nation under heaven," and yet they heard the gospel, says the text, each "in his own language." What occurred then by miraculous power has been taking place ever since by the slower process of providential movements. The word of life is being given to every people in their vernacular.

The Bible has been more generally translated than any other book, having been rendered, in part or as a whole, by the British Society into two hundred and seventy-nine tongues and dialects, and into more than eighty languages by the American Society. Away back to 280 B. C., when the Scriptures (confined then to the Old Testament) existed only in Hebrew, and when in consequence of Alexander's spread of Grecian civilization the Greek language was largely used, it was felt that a translation of the Bible into this tongue was necessary, and the result was the famous Septuagint Version, called Septuagint (meaning seventy) because that number of scholars was supposed, though improbably, to have wrought upon the work.

When Grecian supremacy was succeeded by Roman, the Scriptures were needed in Latin, and accordingly as early as the second century of the Christian era there was a version in this tongue, which Jerome in the fourth century made the basis of what is termed the Vulgate (that is, common), because it was for common use, for ordinary readers who did not understand the original Hebrew and Greek. This translation was violently opposed at first (as all translations have been) on the ground of its being a kind of tampering with God's word, and on the ground of its tending to unsettle the faith of people. But in the course of years it won its way into popular favor.

Then there were versions in Syriac, Ethiopic and in still other ancient languages, and these, being very old, are of great importance in proving the genuineness of the Bible. They show that the sacred writings have entered into the literature of the world, and our religion is thereby given an historic foundation.

The Bible in English is what we are at present specially to consider. Religiously, our Saxon ancestors were not very highly favored. They had to depend upon the clergy for most of their knowledge of the Bible, for there were only fragmentary translations and paraphrases. Their language does not seem much like the present English. When they prayed, "Thy kingdom come," they said, "To cymeth ric thin." Their version of "and his food was locusts and wild honey" ran as follows: "and hys mete waes gaerstapan and wudu-hunig."

1. Not till the time of Wycliffe was the whole Bible translated into English. His rendering of "Thy kingdom come" was "Thi kyngdom cumme to." He was strongly opposed by the ecclesiastics for presuming to give the Holy Book to the laity. They compared it to casting a pearl before swine, but he persevered till, with some assistance, he completed his work in 1380, having made his translation not from the original Hebrew and Greek, but from the Latin Vulgate. Copies of the volume were eagerly sought, although, it being before the invention of printing, a single manuscript copy sold for two hundred dollars of our money. For the merest fragment of a Gospel or an Epistle a whole load of hay would be exchanged.

Wycliffe was sincerely hated by that priestly age, but he died a natural death in 1384. Not till 1415 did the papal authorities see what an opportunity had been missed in not making him a martyr. In that year they did the next best thing. They disinterred his bones, burnt them and committed the ashes to the river Swift to be borne out into the ocean. But, as has been said, those scattered ashes are emblematic of the wide diffusion of the Scriptures which Wycliffe translated.

2. More than a hundred years later Tyndale proposed to have every plough-boy able to read the sacred word. He had to cross to the Continent to make his translation, because, to use his own expression, there was "no place to do it in all England." Even then his steps were dogged by the persecutor. He had to fly from city to city, go under an assumed name and labor in secret. By 1526 he had the satisfaction of seeing the entire New Testament put through the press, for the art of printing was now known. English had by this time become nearly what it is at present, and we readily recognize this sentence, "Geve vs this daye oure dayly breade." The difference is mainly in the spelling. And, so far as that is concerned, our Authorized Version has been changed since 1611, when we find *sin* spelt s-i-nn-e, and *truth*, t-r-u-c-t-h. Aside from the spelling, Tyndale has largely given us our scriptural vocabulary, although some of his words have been changed, and so we say, for instance, dogs where he translated "whelppes." The meaning, of course, is the same with either rendering, and taste determines which is the preferable word. When the Bible is revised it is not changed as to its real substance, but only in the outer dress. The wording of Tyndale, however, has not been greatly altered. He was a fine lin-

THE BIBLE IN ENGLISH. 43

guist, and translating, as he did, from the original Hebrew and Greek, his work surpassed Wycliffe's in value.

Copies were shipped to England, where everything was done to prevent their sale. Spies were on the watch and whole editions were bought up and committed to the flames by the authorities. But an extensive circulation could not be prevented, and there seemed to be no alternative except to cut off the source of supplies. Tyndale himself must be put out of the way, and accordingly he was arrested, having been betrayed by an Englishman who pretended to be his friend, and who had borrowed some money from him on the very morning of the betrayal. He was thrown into prison, whence he wrote a letter beseeching the officer in charge to make him a little more comfortable. He pleaded, to quote his own words, for "a warmer cap, for I suffer extremely from a cold in the head;" for a "warmer coat also, for that which I have is very thin;" and for "a candle in the evening, for it is wearisome to sit alone in the dark." Thus did the noble Tyndale suffer that he might give even the plough-boys of England the word of God. Finally, in 1536 he was strangled, and his body was subsequently given to the flames.

3. After Wycliffe and Tyndale, on the roll of honor and of biblical fame, comes Coverdale, who translated (mostly from Luther's German version and from the Latin Vulgate) the entire Scriptures

in a single year (1535). Thus another version was put into circulation, with a different phraseology, which, for instance, made the dove of Noah's ark to carry the olive-branch, not in the mouth, but " in hir nebb." Public opinion had now begun to change, and Coverdale went so far as to dedicate his Bible to the king, the corrupt Henry the Eighth, who, in the excessive flattery to which that age was given, was likened to Moses, Hezekiah and other Old-Testament worthies.

4. John Rogers (with the pseudonym of Matthew), the famous martyr, who had labored with Tyndale on the Continent in the work of translating the Bible, next prepared a version, which was about two-thirds that of Tyndale and one-third that of Coverdale. This was called Matthew's Bible, and was issued in 1537. So far had the authorities grown favorable that this received the king's " most gracious license." But Henry the Eighth was about as variable with regard to versions as he was with regard to his wives.

5. Accordingly, in 1538 another version was begun under the superintendence of Coverdale at Paris, where the facilities for publishing were better than in London. No sooner was the new work under way at the French capital than the papal power interfered, and it had to be finished in England. Thus in 1539 the Great Bible (prepared chiefly from Matthew's) appeared—sometimes called Cranmer's, on account of a preface which he had in

some editions, but more generally known as the Great Bible, because it was so very large.[5] This was the royal favorite, although Henry before he died seems to have become prejudiced against having the Bible translated at all. He complained that it was becoming too common; or, to use his own expression, he disliked to have it "disputed, rhymed, sung and jangled in every alehouse and tavern." It had become as popular as the Gospel Hymns of to-day. Before any positively backward movement was taken Henry died (1547), and under his successor, Edward the Sixth, during his six and a half years' reign, Bibles were multiplied. All the versions were sold, although Tyndale's seemed to take the lead. "So mightily grew the word of the Lord and prevailed."

6. Then came a change. In 1553 "Bloody Mary" ascended the throne. During her reign of five years there were nearly four hundred martyrs in England. Coverdale narrowly escaped; Rogers (alias Matthew) was burned at the stake, where, says a contemporary (Foxe), he "waved his hand in the flame as though it had been cold water." Multitudes found safety in exile, and to Geneva many of these refugees repaired, and here sprung up another version, perhaps the most important of any yet, unless Tyndale's be an exception. Several distinguished scholars were engaged upon it, bringing it out in full in 1560. This Genevan Bible is sometimes called the "Breeches Bible," because it

says our first parents made themselves not "aprons," but "breeches." This rendering, however, really originated with an earlier fragmentary translation, Caxton's.

The Genevan Version was dedicated to Queen Elizabeth, who had recently succeeded to the English throne, and who was reminded in the preface that it was her duty to crush out the papacy, just as Josiah "burned"—such is the dedicatory language—"the idolatrous priests' bones upon their altars and put to death the false prophets." Those were times when it was worth while to be in the ascendancy, for the principle of toleration was unknown.

The Genevan Version was the first to introduce the present verse arrangement, having borrowed the idea from the Greek text of Stephens, who made the minute divisions in 1551 during a horseback ride from Paris to Lyons. This version at once took high rank, and it really had superior merit. It seemed likely to crowd out even the Great Bible, which had been considered on the whole the best, especially in the higher circles of life. The Great Bible was the one used in the churches, but it was so very great, so large and unwieldy, it did not find its way into the home. Now, the Genevan, with its brief explanatory notes (very essential in those days), seemed just adapted to family use. Its circulation accordingly increased more and more. The churchmen became alarmed, not liking the obvious opposition of its notes to episcopacy.

7. Recognizing that they could never make the bulky Great Bible popular, they took steps to prepare another version, which was a revision of the Great, and which was published in 1568. This is sometimes called the "Treacle Bible," because of the translation (Jer. 8 : 22), " Is there no tryacle in Gilead?" where we have "balm;" but "triacle" also occurs in Coverdale (1535). The more common name is the "Bishops' Bible," because it was the work of several bishops, among whom parts were distributed. It gave us the word *church*, which before had generally been translated "congregation." This was the version which had the ecclesiastical sanction, but Queen Elizabeth herself did not cast the royal influence decidedly in favor of any version, all the versions being allowed. It was enough that she took sides against the papists without antagonizing any wing of the Protestants.

8. Elizabeth's persecution of the Roman Catholics resulted in their leaving the country in large numbers. Many of them took refuge at Rheims and Douay, and from these places came the Romish Bible—the New Testament in 1582 from Rheims, and the Old Testament in 1609 from Douay. The translators acknowledged that they did not approve of the Scriptures being rendered "in our mother tongue," but that they were forced into the ungrateful task because of what they termed the "impure versions" and "profane translations" of the Protestants. They translated from the Latin Vulgate,

which they rather singularly pronounced "better than the Greek text itself," although Greek was the original language of part of the Bible. This version renders "penance" for "repentance," and according to it "the hands of priesthood," and not of "presbytery," were laid upon young Timothy in ordination. While there are these grave defects, the Catholic or Douay Bible has some more accurate renderings than the other versions, as where it is said that the lamps of the foolish virgins were *going* out, not *gone* out, as in our Authorized Version; and the New Revision has adopted this improvement.

9. The next version was that of 1611, under King James. This was made to secure uniformity. Even under the preceding sovereign, Elizabeth, a bill was introduced "for reducing diversities of Bibles." It, however, was not carried through. Under James the feeling grew in favor of an "authorized" version. The king disliked all existing translations, and particularly the Genevan (which was the most used), because of its independent notes, which savored, he said, "too much of traitorous conceits." One bishop objected to any more versions, on the ground that "if every man's humor should be followed, there would be no end of translating." But he was overruled in his opinion, and soon forty-seven (fifty-four were at first named) of the ripest scholars of England were at work. Both the great universities, Oxford and

THE BIBLE IN ENGLISH. 49

Cambridge, were represented, as well as as both Puritans and Churchmen, to whom respectively the Genevan and the Bishops' versions were very dear. The movement was begun in 1604, and the final result was reached in 1611, although the actual time spent was a little more than three years. Thus there came into being our so-called "Authorized Version," combining the excellences of all the previous versions which the translators declared to be "sound for substance." Theirs was undoubtedly an improvement upon any of the preceding. It of course encountered opposition, and for some forty years the Genevan especially disputed the field with it, but it gradually gained ground till it displaced all others.

But it was not perfect, and was not so considered from the outset. Under Cromwell another revision was seriously proposed, but the proposition came to nothing on account of the sudden dissolution of Parliament.

10. After a lapse of two hundred and fifty years, however, it is not strange that modern scholarship entered upon the new revision in 1870, the best scholars of both England and America, without distinction of sect, co-operating. The result of their most careful labors through many more years than have ever been given to a similar work before is in our hands in the Revised Version, the New Testament appearing in 1881, and the Old in 1885. There are certainly many improvements. The same

word when evidently used in the same sense is no longer translated by a dozen different, and sometimes confusing, terms. Old manuscripts which have come to light since 1611 have enabled us to get what is more nearly the actual word of God. We have also secured more accurate, if not more euphonious, renderings. Poetical quotations are more impressive; the Psalms appear more what they are—"songs of Zion"—when they are given, as they are, in their metrical form. For such and other reasons the Revised Version has been given a wide welcome. It is being largely introduced into our institutions of learning, and it is being used more and more in churches. Time alone can determine whether, like other improved versions, it will eventually come into general favor, or whether it will be still further improved before it displaces the version which has been used for two centuries and a half.

The fear, at first entertained, of the unsettling influence of a revision of the Bible has been dissipated by a growing intelligence. Faith is strengthened by the grand unity underlying the minor diversities of the various versions, and by the scholarly and painstaking endeavors in successive centuries to get at the exact meaning of the words spoken of old in Hebrew and Greek by prophets and apostles.

The Bible in English has a bright prospect when we consider with Gladstone "the future of English-speaking races." This statesman has recently estimated those who will speak English in the year 2000 at eight hundred and forty millions. He calculates that the United States alone by 1987 will have five hundred and fifty to five hundred and eighty milllions who will speak the language of Shakespeare. He thinks that a century hence those who speak English may outnumber those using all the other European tongues. This signifies a great deal as to the future of our English Bible. Already, says Dr. N. G. Clark, "the English language, saturated with Christian ideas, gathering up into itself the best thought of all the ages, is the great agent of Christian civilization throughout the world, at this moment affecting the destinies and moulding the character of half the human race." If an Anglo-Saxon minority is having such a mighty influence, what will not its coming majority accomplish? The Bible in English is destined to dominate the world, to be largely instrumental in its conversion. Let us therefore treasure this book which has come down through the ages by being translated into new languages when the old have died; which has sought and found the latest and very best expression when languages have been modified by time; which has increasingly appeared in all the tongues of earth, elevating every nation where it has been read in the vernacular; and which has with special care been wrought into English, the tongue that most of all is to be used round the globe.

CHAPTER IV.

THE INSPIRATION OF THE BIBLE.

"Every scripture inspired of God is also profitable for teaching, for reproof, for correction, for instruction which is in righteousness."—2 TIM. 3: 16.

THIS text gives us for a theme the Inspiration of the Bible.

1. In the first place, what are some of the scriptural representations of this subject? The writers of the Old Testament are constantly saying, "Thus saith the Lord." David's words in one of the Psalms are quoted in Hebrews as the language of the Holy Ghost. Paul refers to the Spirit of God speaking by different prophets. Peter says that the prophets were "moved by the Holy Ghost." Nor did the apostles consider their own words as less authoritative. Paul tells the Corinthians that what he writes them is "the commandment of the Lord." He professes to speak "not in words which man's wisdom teacheth, but which the Spirit teacheth." In fact, all the apostles make the salvation of men dependent on faith in the doctrines which they preached. Still higher authority we find in the Saviour himself. As regards the Old Testament,

THE INSPIRATION OF THE BIBLE. 53

he again and again refers to it to confirm even what he says; and as regards the New, when he commissioned the disciples to teach he said, "It is not ye that speak, but the Spirit of your Father that speaketh in you." All Christians, then, can feel that in the Bible they have the word of God.

2. To take a step in advance, Does the supernatural enter into the idea of inspiration? It would seem that the writers of the Bible had more than ordinary spiritual illumination. They spoke with an authority more than human. No preacher at the present time can reasonably claim to be taught by direct revelation, nor can he call what he urges a "commandment of the Lord;" and yet an apostle could and did do this. We never preface a remark with a genuine "Thus saith the Lord." We may possibly venture it with the sanction of Scripture, but never as intending to imply that we received the communication direct from Heaven. Our preaching has power only so far as we can say, Thus saith Scripture. The apostles and prophets could go back of the written word, and say with all the force that comes from a personal, face-to-face knowledge, "Thus saith the Lord." Here, therefore, is a distinctive characteristic of a true inspiration. All God's people are inspired in a certain way, but divine authority is connected only with those who can utter words breathed from an inspiration which is supernatural. This test separates the Scriptures from all other writings. The authors of

the Old Testament are either professedly God's spokesmen (and they sustain their claim by their life and work) or they are recognized as such by those whose divine inspiration is undoubted. The Old Testament as a whole is repeatedly appealed to by the Saviour even to give weight to his own God-spoken words. As to the New Testament, it was composed by those who had the promise of being led by the Spirit "into all the truth." Inspiration is thus more than the enlightenment common to believers. For this reason the Epistles just after the apostolic age are excluded from the canon. One is impressed with the descent he has made when he compares Paul with Ignatius, and the apostolic writings in general with the earliest patristic literature. It has well been said that the New Testament "is not like a city of modern Europe, which subsides through suburban gardens and groves and mansions into the open country around, but like an Eastern city in the desert, from which the traveler passes by a single step into a barren waste." In the Bible alone we find the truth at first hand. Ordinary Christians get their knowledge at second hand. They have to search the Scriptures, they must use instrumentalities—instrumentalities furnished by holy men of old who talked with Jehovah himself, and so received the truth from God's own lips. Such is inspiration—not when the soul through provided avenues goes after God, but when the human spirit touches the great Spirit, feeling the thrill of personal contact, inbreathing the pure truth till it is not Paul-inspired, but God-inspired.

And while the faculties of the sacred writers seem sometimes to have been merely quickened and elevated as they related what they saw or what they learned through human testimony, they certainly had also an illumination of a higher kind than this; as Paul had when he received "revelations of the Lord," and when he solemnly declared of the gospel, "Neither did I receive it from man, nor was I taught it, but it came to me through revelation of Jesus Christ." God might grant this supernatural inspiration to men now as of old, so that the same weight should be attached to their words. This is possible, and yet as a matter of fact it seems not to be done. If one speaks with the authority of a Paul, we can pay him the same deference, provided that he shows the signs of an apostle. Let him work miracles, and then we may consider the propriety of enlarging the canon. We can test his apostolic claims, as we say with Luther, "Send him into the graveyard, and let him raise the dead."

3. While inspiration is supernatural, it is not always or mainly a process of dictation. Holy *men* spake as moved by the Spirit; they were men, and not machines. Their faculties were not generally overpowered with the divine, so much as they were stimulated and exalted. Sometimes, indeed, one was so filled with the Spirit that he wrote in a

strain more or less mysterious to himself even, for we learn from the first chapter of the first letter of Peter that prophets searched into the meaning of their own utterances. Probably the orator in the fervor of address sweeps along with a grandeur and an eloquence surprising to himself in his cooler moments. This may partially account for Peter's statement that the prophets studied their own predictions, but this explanation does not give the whole truth. We must distinguish between the inspiration of revelation and of elevation. The former is that of a man who did not know whether he was "in the body" or "out of the body"—a condition of things making somewhat pertinent the familiar illustration of a musical instrument played upon and giving out unconsciously the harmonies of its masterful manipulator. But even the chief of the apostles intimated that this was an exceptional experience, and he seemed desirous of being regarded as a man among men, with the common passions of humanity, yet so dominated by the Spirit as to be one of the Lord's authoritative teachers. "There are diversities of gifts," he said, "but the same Spirit." He recognized that individual peculiarities are preserved. Inspiration did not become merely mechanical, so as to destroy personality, but it used different persons in the way in which they were variously constituted mentally. We see this to be an actual fact with regard to biblical authors. The logical Paul shows his power of reasoning in every sentence. The devotional John is more emotional and meditative in what he says. The matter-of-fact James writes plainly and practically. The Bible is a very natural as well as supernatural book. It is not a collection of rhythmical, stilted verses from the frenzied head of a Delphic priestess. It is the product of men speaking out from the fullness of sanctified personalities. Individuality is not suppressed; it is stimulated, developed and glorified. The apostles were not mere pens in the hands of an overruling Spirit. They wrote according to their own natures, being, as the chief of them said, "men of like passions" with the rest of mankind. Their inspiration was not automatic, but pervasive and energizing.

4. We are next led to inquire the extent of inspiration. Is it plenary, extending to the words? The fact seems to be that all the sacred writers were inspired, but in different degrees. The strictest inspirationist must admit that the eighth chapter of Romans has more of the spiritual element than the first chapter of Chronicles. The difference between the Psalms and genealogical tables is apparent. Baxter considered portions of the Bible to be like the nails and hair as related to the human body. Nevertheless, we must regard even the commonplace parts of the Scriptures as inspired, unless we consider inspiration a kind of fit. We can hardly suppose the apostle Paul to have been an

ordinary mortal when he wrote his friendly salutations to various persons named, and then suddenly to have become an entirely different being when he poured forth his living thoughts. Inspiration is not a momentary assistance, when the Spirit wishes to be eloquent; it is a controlling force in all the life. The inspired penmen had within them a vital principle. They were not spasmodically seized by the Spirit to communicate some truth, and then released to follow their own pleasure. They were so possessed and penetrated by the spiritual that everything they wrote had weight. If a great and good man should write us a letter, we would not reject as useless the superscription because it might not have in it the fire of genius. The whole letter would be a treasure, though some parts might be better than others. We would not be disposed to run a pruning-knife through it and to throw aside the less important portions. We would not be so finical as that. Even so the whole Bible is inspired, though it may not be all equally precious, and we are not going to choose and reject its contents in accordance with any superfine critical spirit. The beauty of the Bible is that it treats of the historical. It shows the working of God in history. It is not a body of doctrine claiming to have been let down from heaven all cut and dried at a definite past period. It grew out of circumstances from time to time. It has to do with facts, with actual events, and with God manifest therein, and hence it takes hold of us with all the force of tremendous reality. The oak, grand and strong, has insignificant outgrowths, but it is the same sap which courses through the trunk and through its smallest branches. The glorious old Bible may have comparatively unimportant parts, but it is the same spirit which gives life to the whole.

In saying that inspiration extends to all the contents of Scripture are we committed to verbal inspiration? In a certain sense, yes. Words express thought, and it would be of little avail to maintain spiritual help in getting the truth, if the truth must, after all, be communicated in words bungling and inaccurate. As Van Oosterzee says: "If the true poetic spirit enables one to seize at once, and as by intuition, the exact and only suitable word for that which one desires to express, how much more shall the power of the Holy Spirit!" That is, if poetic inspiration is so felicitous in catching the precise word, divine inspiration cannot surely have less power of expression.

5. One more question arises: Does the doctrine of inspiration, as has been set forth, exclude absolutely all errors from the Bible? Matthew, for instance, in citing an Old-Testament prophecy gives it from Jeremiah, whereas it is found in Zechariah. Apparently this, unless it is an error of transcribers, is a slip of memory. There are other alleged inaccuracies of a trifling nature, and, granting that the explanations offered are not altogether satis-

factory, our faith need not be disturbed. The disciples were promised the Spirit to lead them into "all the truth," and the truth indicated is spiritual truth, the truth of the gospel. The authority of a New-Testament writer in morals and religion can hardly be thought to be impaired by a possible failure to name the right author of a certain sentiment. An argument in favor of the equal rights of blacks and whites would not be invalidated by an illustration drawn from some slave's condition in Georgia, even though it might be discovered afterward that said slave had lived not in Georgia, but in Alabama. Any trivial inaccuracy (if such there be) on the part of the biblical authors does not affect their reliability as regards the plan of salvation taught them by the Lord himself or by direct revelation.

So if it should be established that Old-Testament writers shared the false astronomical notions of their contemporaries, and that they even gave expression incidentally to a mistaken astronomy, they could still be infallible religious guides. Baronius long ago said with fine force, "Scripture is not given to make us acquainted with the course of heavenly bodies, but with the way to heaven itself." Inspired Scripture is profitable, according to the text, for what? To inform us upon Huxley's molecular changes? No. To give scientific explanation of the Copernican system of the universe? No. To give a description of trilobites and brachiopods?

No. But "profitable for teaching, for reproof, for correction, for instruction which is in righteousness." It gives us a development theory, to be sure, but it is Christian development—how to grow in grace till the stature of perfect manhood in Christ Jesus is reached. The first chapter in Genesis is not meant to teach geology. The great thought there is not, In the beginning — protoplasm, or "frog-spawn" as Carlyle said; not, In the beginning—a fire-mist; but back of all this, "In the beginning—God created the heaven and the earth." A geological error, if proved, need not unsettle our faith in the reliability of the Bible within the sphere of religion. A first-class doctor to whom we should be willing to entrust our lives might within the domain of the law make mistakes without any discredit to him as a physician. A pilot might be entirely safe in conducting us past danger in a rushing stream, even if he called the obstruction in the river-bed trap-rock when he should have said sand-stone. The Bible can be an unerring religious guide even though it might say Jeremiah when it should have said Zechariah, and though it might make some astronomical or geological or historical error. Yet alleged errors do not always turn out to be such. Nearly all, if not quite all, difficulties in the Bible have been satisfactorily explained or harmonized without admitting that there have been mistakes of any kind. And if there is still an occasional obstacle to entire faith, we may well wait for further light before positively pronouncing against the infallibility of the Bible along all lines.

Take the case of the proper title of Sergius Paulus, the governor of the island of Cyprus. Luke, in the *Acts*, called him "proconsul," whereas, it used to be averred, he should have said "propraetor," for Cyprus was an imperial and not a senatorial province. Both Strabo and Dion Cassius name Cyprus an imperial district, and its governor should therefore have been called propraetor, so formerly said those who would discredit Luke. Christians used to be troubled by the apparent inaccuracy of Luke in saying "proconsul," and the eminent Grotius reluctantly admitted, on the authority of the two pagan writers quoted, that the author of the *Acts* had fallen into an error. It was as if one should pretend to write the history of the present, and should speak of Mr. Cleveland as Senator instead of President. Of course, Christians were distressed, and they resorted to all sorts of ingenious explanations. But by and by in the same secular historian, Dion Cassius, it was discovered that while Augustus did hold Cyprus as an imperial province for a while, he exchanged it for another district, and it thus became a senatorial province, and proconsul became the proper title for its governor, and Luke, after all, was shown to be correct. To make the matter still surer, coins of the time have been found, and these call the rulers of Cyprus procon-

THE INSPIRATION OF THE BIBLE.   63

suls. Still further, General Cesnola in his recent excavations at Cyprus came upon a coin bearing the inscription, "in the proconsulship of Paulus," who may have been the very one named by Luke. So completely has been established even the historical accuracy of the author of the *Acts* in speaking of the proconsul Sergius Paulus. More light may clear up other difficulties, and we should be slow to admit errors of any kind in God's word. We can afford to hang up present perplexities and to wait, while yet there is always that impregnable position, to which we can if necessary fall back, of the infallibility of the Bible in all spiritual matters at least.

We thus have in the Scriptures the word of God, supernaturally though not mechanically inspired, pervaded throughout by the Spirit, even to the words so far as these are essential to main ideas, while at the same time any possible minor mistakes on side issues need not weaken our faith in the trustworthiness of those whose grand theme is the gospel of Jesus Christ.

There is a human and a divine element in inspiration. The exact relations of the two seem incapable of precise statement. The question is one which is trying the minds of the present generation, and in the end the efforts may be no more satisfactory than have been the attempts to define the exact relations between the human and the divine in the God-man. We can be thankful for the human element in the Bible, as we are for the human nature united with the divine nature in Christ. It gives point of contact. "In all points tempted like as we are," "touched with the feeling of our infirmities." There we have the human in the Lord Jesus. It is similar with the inspired writers, who were men of like passions with us. They were not spiritual automatons, different from us in every particular. They had more of the divine rather than less of the human. They were men, but men inspired, and, reading them, spirit touches spirit till we are all aglow, even as burned the hearts of the two disciples when to them were opened the Scriptures.

CHAPTER V.

THE BIBLE AND THE MIRACULOUS.

"Believe me for the very works' sake."—John 14:11.

CHRIST here appeals to the evidence of his miracles. Anciently, the fact of miracles seems not to have been questioned. Even the Pharisees did not dispute their occurrence. They only claimed that Christ performed them by being in league with Satan. But in modern times the miraculous is denied altogether. Nor is the disbelief confined to revilers—to such men as Paine and Voltaire, who attacked the Bible bitterly, who did not want it to be true because of their immoral lives. The unbelief has extended to persons of good character, to those who admire Christianity when stripped of the supernatural, to those who are honest in their investigations, who have fine ability, and whose scientific attainments, it may be, are of a high order. They say, as did Nicodemus in a different connection, "How can these things be?" They consider the miraculous as neither probable nor possible.

1. First, as to the possibility of miracles. Renan says, "The supernatural is impossible." Without

considering any miracles in detail, let us see in general if they are incredible, for if they are the Bible, which deals so largely in them, must go to the wall.

The rationalist explains them away. He says that Christ gave sight to the blind, not by a miracle, but by his skill as an oculist. He did not really raise Lazarus from the dead, but he recovered him from a swoon. The trouble with this rationalizing is that sometimes the miracles are not so wonderful as the explanations. It taxes us more to believe the latter than the former. Paulus, for instance, at the beginning of this century said that Peter did not catch the fish with the piece of money in its mouth, but he caught a fish and sold it for the amount named. He read the record very carefully, " Go thou to the sea, and cast a hook, and take up the fish that first cometh up; and when thou hast *opened his mouth—*" There! said this rationalist, it is more natural to suppose not that Peter opened the fish's mouth and took out the money, but that he opened his own mouth, crying the fish for sale. The picture is more vivid than dignified as we imagine the apostle, in accordance with this conception, walking the streets of Capernaum and calling, " Nice fresh fish! just caught from the lake!" The story, taken literally, is a great deal more credible than any such fantastic explanation. Miracles are not so difficult that we have to resort to any such makeshifts of interpretation.

The possibility of miracles has sometimes been illustrated in this way—that they are the result of natural laws unknown to all but the miracle-worker. This is the theory: God so formed the universe in the very beginning that it should at intervals produce miracles. The common illustration is that of a machine made to turn out square numbers millions of times, while after that it gives forth a cube, and then only squares till the machine wears out. There are two ways of accounting for the solitary cube number: the maker of the machine may have directly interfered at the moment, or he may have provided for the change in the original construction of his fine piece of mechanism. Thus it is with God's machine, the universe, which generally produces ordinary events, but which once in a while gives forth the miraculous. How is it done? Why, by no immediate interference of God; the whole thing was planned by him from the very outset. A hidden spring was made to act at long intervals, and if we could see this spring miracles would seem perfectly natural.

We may illustrate in another way: We may suppose little creatures which live for only two or three hours standing before a clock. There is a tradition among them that the clock once rang out a terrible alarm, startling all that heard. But all of them now alive never heard anything except a tick! tick! tick! or perhaps the striking of the hour. Some of them do not believe that there ever was an alarm. Fellow-insects have come and gone and have heard nothing of the sort. Meanwhile the clock runs on until it comes to the point for which the alarm was set, and all at once there is a whir and a clatter and a racket, such as has not been heard for several generations, and little unbelievers are convinced of what through their ignorance they had doubted. So we stand before God's great clock denying that there ever was the miraculous. And yet it is not incredible that there was a secret spring made to ring out an alarm at certain periods—that there came after a long lapse of time the miraculous to arrest the attention of mankind and to wake them up to the higher ends of human existence.

A more poetic illustration is furnished by the century-plant. The first year it has no blossom, nor has it the second year, nor the third, nor the twentieth, nor the seventieth; and then the owner dies. His son keeps the plant. He is asked if it ever blooms. "Oh no!" he replies, "that is not its nature." The eightieth year comes, the ninetieth, the hundredth, and lo, it blossoms! The credulous mind might consider it a miracle in the strictest sense—that is, something supernaturally produced on the spot. But the botanist knows that the plant blooms once a century from natural causes. In like manner, the course of history runs for a hundred years, two hundred, five hundred, and at the end of a millennium there is an age of miracles. But there is nothing incredibly miraculous; in the natural order of events the time has come for the blossom—that is all. The world is made to bloom for a while in accordance with the eternal purpose of God.

The hidden-law theory, thus variously illustrated, at least serves to show that miracles are not absolutely impossible on account of the apparent fixity of natural laws; for we do not know what all these laws are or what provision may have been made for rising emergencies. But the Church in general does not hold to so mechanical a view of the world as has just been indicated. It is not necessary to maintain that the universe was so *constituted* as to produce the miraculous at certain prearranged epochs.

It is easier for most men to believe that God produces the miracles at the time by a direct act of power. Why should he not be able to do this? Why should he not be able to counteract natural law? It is being done constantly—not in a way to be termed miraculous, because it is an every-day occurrence, but in a way which illustrates the miraculous. The chemical law of decay is suspended by the preservative law of salt. The law of gravity draws the stone to the earth, but you counteract that law when you lift it from the ground and hurl it into the air. There is no violation of law in such instances, but only a suspension. The watchmaker can prevent the wheels of a watch from running, but let him loosen his hold upon the delicate machinery and it runs again all right. Why cannot God similarly interfere in his works, suspending or counteracting natural laws at will? He can, and when he does a miracle is the result. Dr. A. T. Pierson uses this figure: "I have a watch here; when wound up it runs straight forward until it needs rewinding. . . . Yet when I find it is too fast I move the hands backward—I interrupt the usual movement, but I violate no law. The watch could not have turned back its own hands and corrected itself, but a superior intelligence interferes for a proper end. . . . As I examine more minutely into the structure of this delicate piece of mechanism, I observe a remarkable fact: the maker of this watch has *made provision for just such a reversal of that law* by which both minute- and hour-hands move only forward. He has provided for a backward movement when the intelligent owner chooses."

So that miracles are possible to Omnipotence, either after the manner of a higher law of which we at present are ignorant, or, more likely, through the suspension and balancing and manipulation of laws already known, but not known in all their wonderful power of combination to produce results. Twenty years ago it would have seemed a miracle for the human voice to be heard at a distance of fifty or a hundred miles. But there has come such a knowledge of the laws of electricity and sound that by the telephone there can be vocal communication at ranges of distance once deemed impossible. Who, then, will limit the Omnipotent and Omniscient, and say that God cannot by his perfect understanding of natural laws and by his almighty power work miracles? "Since," says the geologist Dawson, "science itself enables men to work miracles absolutely impossible and unintelligible to the ignorant, we may readily believe that the Almighty can still more profoundly modify and rearrange his own laws and forces. Viewed in this way," adds this eminent scientist, "a miracle is a most natural thing, and to be expected in any case where events great and momentous in a spiritual sense are transpiring." Gladstone in his review of *Robert Elsmere* has given expression to a similar thought. "There is," he says, "an extraneous force of will which acts upon matter in derogation of laws purely physical, or alters the balance of those laws among themselves. It can be neither philosophical nor scientific to proclaim the impossibility of a miracle until philosophy or science shall have determined a limit beyond which this extraneous force of will, so familiar to our experience, cannot act upon or deflect the natural order." Even Huxley, though declaring that supernatural Christianity is "doomed to fall," says, "No one is entitled to say *a priori* that any given so-called miraculous event is impossible." That is a recent admission of his; so that the possibility of miracles would seem to be beyond controversy.

2. We come thus, in the second place, to the probability of miracles. This Huxley denies on the ground of insufficient evidence. We have all read Hume's famous argument, which may be stated as follows: On the one side there is the evidence of certain witnesses; on the other is the testimony of universal experience which declares the laws of nature to be unalterable. Those who witness to the miraculous having taken place are few as compared with the multitudes who testify to the unbroken succession of natural laws. So that it is a question of probabilities—it is a hundred or a thousand or several thousand saying they have *seen* supernatural events, while millions upon millions have seen, and so will admit, only natural events. It is more probable that the few should be wrong than the many. Such is the position taken, but it cannot be sustained. If ten worthy persons passing along the street should say that they saw a certain picture in a store-window, and a hundred others should unite in saying that they did not notice it, and therefore that it could not be there, we would believe the ten rather than the hundred.

To use a familiar illustration: Suppose a people living in the tropics never to have heard of ice, but a half dozen of them, good, reliable men, take passage northward. Returning, they tell their fellow-countrymen that water sometimes becomes solid, so that it can be walked upon. Improbable enough, those tropical people might say; it is against nature.

Thus the ignorant natives would all be arrayed against the six travelers, and could claim a preponderance of witnesses, but they would be wrong just the same. What if for eighteen centuries no miracle has been seen by any who have inhabited this earth? That weighs as nothing against five hundred who did witness miracles in the first century of the Christian era.

The miraculous would seem to be probable, instead of improbable, when we think of *the ends to be gained.* There have been in the course of human history occasions apparently at least requiring divine intervention. Horace, the old Roman poet, had the correct idea when he said, "Let not a god intervene unless there be a knot worth his untying." Well, there have been just such emergencies.

In Old-Testament times the great endeavor was to establish the true doctrine of one personal God. The tendency was to deify the forces of nature, giving gods innumerable. How could this polytheism be overcome by monotheism? How could people be made to believe in a God over and above nature, rather than in numerous deities identical with nature in its various aspects? We have no appreciation of the great issue involved. The prevailing religions were polytheistic. The whole atmosphere was unfavorable to the truth of one personal God. The divine One had, so to speak, to manifest himself: he could not have gotten the attention without miracles. Not that he performed them every day.

There are hundreds of years at a time devoid of the miraculous. We forget that Bible history is fragmentary, containing only the striking epochs. Even in the scriptural history which we have, while there are miracles scattered along here and there, they *abounded* only at two critical periods under the old dispensation: in the time of Moses, when the new religion was to be established, and in the time of Elijah, when it seemed likely to go down before idolatry. God came in with the miraculous at both these periods, because they were great crises when the true religion needed special nourishing. When we reflect upon what was at stake, when we remember it was then being determined whether we to-day should be worshiping the God of heaven or bowing down to stocks and stones, we can see the reasonableness of the divine intervention.

The advent of Christ in the new dispensation was another great epoch. When we learn of the almost universal skepticism that existed nineteen centuries ago, the old faiths everywhere crumbling, and when we read of the shocking immoralities that were practiced, not secretly, but openly, not in the slums of society, but in the very temples of worship, —when we have knowledge of all this, and then remember that a single individual who was cradled in a manger, and who as he grew up worked at the carpenter's trade,—when we recollect that this one Person of humble birth and training was to revolutionize the world, we can understand why the miraculous should be used. It is what we should expect, and never could Christianity have become the mighty power that it is had there not been the supernatural to give it impetus in the beginning. If there were not miracles to aid in its establishment, a miracle is required to explain its widening influence down the ages, until now nothing else can be compared with it in grandeur of onward movement as it sweeps in triumph round the globe. The gifted author of *Christianity and Science,* Dr. A. P. Peabody, writes eloquently of this advance without retrogression since the first century. " What do we see since that age ?" he asks; and then answers, " Progress, but no decline. Dawn, sunrise, high morning, but no receding of the shadow on the sundial. Barbaric irruptions that fertilize when they threaten to destroy. Dark ages, like those dreary spring-days whose drenching rains are the harbinger of all that is gladdening in garden, field and orchard —ages during which humane principles are taking root, institutions and habits of charity and mercy springing into being, slavery melting away and vanishing. There has not been since the Christian era a century than which we can say that the preceding century was better. . . . When we see that belief in such a religion, in such a Saviour, though mingled with puerilities, superstitions and absurdities, has proved the mightiest force in the moral universe, alone not yielding to the law of decline and exhaustion to which all other forces have succumbed, it becomes in the highest degree probable that mankind needed such a religion, such a Saviour; and if so the miracles that attended its promulgation and his mission were in themselves antecedently probable."

The miraculous, then, is even probable, both in the old and in the new dispensation, when we recollect that it was a life-and-death struggle between monotheism and polytheism—between a personal God and deified nature, and when we recollect that it was a contest between a pure Christianity and an immoral skepticism, and when we see the victory attained in both these great conflicts.

But when the truth was thoroughly established in each case, it was left to a natural development and the miraculous was withdrawn. Chrysostom of the fourth century (the "golden-mouthed," as he was called) expresses this beautifully when he says: "As . . . a husbandman, having lately committed a young tree to the bosom of the earth, counts it worthy, being yet tender, of much attention, on every side fencing it round, protecting it with stones and thorns, so that it neither may be torn up by the winds, nor harmed by the cattle, nor injured by any other injury; but when he sees that it is fast-rooted and has sprung up on high, he takes away the defences, since now the tree can defend itself from any such wrong; thus has it been in the matter of our faith. When it was newly planted, while it was yet tender, great attention was bestowed on it on every side. But after it was fixed and rooted and sprung up on high, after it had filled all the world, Christ . . . took away the defences." In other words, the miraculous no longer hedged it round. Let us be grateful that the precious gospel was thus nurtured. It was planted, the Saviour said, the least of all seeds, but, to paraphrase from one of the Psalms, it has taken deep root and filled all lands. The hills are covered with the shadow of it, and the boughs thereof are like goodly cedars, stretching from sea to sea. Verily, this cannot be the product of natural development alone. The miraculous is needed to explain the marvelous growth.

In conclusion, He who said, "Believe me for the very works' sake," is the One to whom are to be ascribed the works of creation, and these surely witness to miraculous power. "All things were made by him," says John. He therefore spoke into being our solar system, with its central sun and circling planets and revolving moons. He called into existence each of those other almost innumerable suns, like ours centres (only vastly larger) around which wheel other planetary bodies with their bright satellites. He flung forth into boundless space that mass of stars concerning which the astronomer Young declares, "Its diameter must be as great as twenty or thirty thousand light-years—how much greater we cannot even guess;" and concerning which also Proctor writes, "Light reaches this earth from unseen orbs so far away that the journey over the vast abysses separating us from them has not been completed in less than millions of years." He swung into their vast orbits the colored suns, those blazing constellations with all the beautiful tints of the rainbow. Notwithstanding this marvelous manifestation through the visible of "his everlasting power and divinity," we, creatures of the dust and of a day, stand up and debate whether he can work a miracle, whether he can control what he has made with his own hands. May the wonderful works of creation lead us to believe in the miraculous works of the Lord of glory! and may the latter make us believe in Him himself who built the skies! Then when we come to die there will be no volume like that which has taught us these things, and there will be no chapter like that which contains our text and which contains the revelation of the heavenly mansions. Our feeling at the dying hour will be that of Sir Walter Scott, who, as he neared his end, asked Lockhart to read to him, and when the latter inquired, "Out of what book?" the reply was, "Need you ask? there is but one;" and thereupon the Bible was brought, and the chapter read and listened to with delight was this fourteenth of John, which says, "In my Father's house are many mansions," and which says, "Believe me for the very works' sake."

CHAPTER VI.

FORMIDABLE OBJECTIONS TO THE BIBLE.

" Where wast thou when I laid the foundations of the earth?
Declare, if thou hast understanding.
* * * * * *
Doubtless, thou knowest, for thou wast then born,
And the number of thy days is great!"—Job 38: 4, 21.

NOT infrequently there is a person who challenges the truthfulness of God's word, who questions some of the more marvelous things related in the Scriptures. We will frankly consider certain of the more formidable objections to the Bible, and by seeing the light which can be thrown even upon these, perhaps we will have our faith sufficiently strengthened not to stumble at every apparent obstacle, or at least we will have learned not to accept the dictum of the infidel who thinks he knows more of the history of the past than the men who lived therein. He has not the least hesitation in denying the occurrence of events which the Bible vouches for through living witnesses of the time. He is perfectly sure the scriptural narrative does not correspond to the actual facts. Every once in a while he gets tripped up; still, he keeps on impugning the statements of the sacred historians. A little of the modesty inculcated by our text would be to the advantage of the supercilious unbeliever:

> "Where wast thou when I laid the foundations of the earth? Declare, if thou hast understanding.
>
> * * * * * *
>
> Doubtless, thou knowest, for thou wast then born, And the number of thy days is great!"

1. The most brilliant infidel of the day describes the Holy Land as "one-fifth the size of Illinois— a frightful country, covered with rocks and desolation. There never was an agent in Chicago that would not have blushed with shame to have described that land as flowing with milk and honey." Was, then, the description thus given in Exodus of Palestine overdrawn? The expression, of course, was a poetic one to indicate great fruitfulness. The Roman poet Ovid, who died during the lifetime of Christ, has a similar idea when he writes thus of the Golden Age:

> "Here rivers of milk, there rivers of nectar, were flowing, And from the green of the oaks the yellow honey was dropping."

But the trouble is, that the Holy Land is singularly barren, stony and unproductive. That is, however, no evidence that it has always been so. For one thing, the timber has been all cut down, and the bad results of that we of modern times know.

FORMIDABLE OBJECTIONS. 81

Indeed, governments are now offering premiums for the planting of trees, and New York is discussing the necessity of preserving the vast forests of the Adirondacks if the Empire State is not to lose its fertility. Thus the present sterility of Palestine can be accounted for; the trees are largely gone. Besides, there are on the hillsides ruins showing that anciently terraces were made use of for the better cultivation of the land. That theory, says the objector, may be plausible enough, and may be correct, but is there any absolute proof that the soil was once productive? Yes, the Bible. But its statements are denied, although why this should be is not exactly clear. Why will some admit at once the truth of what pagans write? Are they so much more trustworthy than holy men of old?

But since our infidels prefer other than scriptural authorities, they shall be satisfied. Tacitus, of the end of the first and of the beginning of the second century, says expressly of Palestine: "The soil is rich." Josephus, a contemporary of the apostles, says of Galilee that the "soil is universally rich and fruitful. . . . Moreover, the cities lie here very thick, and the very many villages there are here are everywhere so full of people, by the richness of their soil, that the very least of them contain above fifteen thousand inhabitants. . . . It supplies men with the principal fruits, with grapes and figs continually, during ten months of the year." A Chicago land-agent would not need to blush much over such a possession. Nay, he could put up his posters that it does actually flow with milk and honey, for Josephus goes on to observe of Judæa and Samaria: "By reason also of the excellent grass they have, their cattle yield more *milk* than do those in other places." Then if that agent could have only controlled the land in the vicinity of Jericho, he could have advertised, on the authority of Josephus, that "it will not be easy to light on any climate in the habitable earth that can well be compared to it;" while he could have also quoted from the Jewish writer: "This country withal produces *honey* from bees." Milk and honey! Yet our smooth-tongued infidel, who knows more of the past than the people who lived then, says, "There never was an agent in Chicago that would not have blushed with shame to have described that land as flowing with milk and honey." This is only a sample of the way in which historical facts are set aside by the superficial and unscholarly infidelity which is making so much noise through the press and from the platform. Even if the Bible cannot always be immediately verified by secular authorities, that is no reason why we should pronounce it false. We do not know everything; our age is not so great that we have personal knowledge of centuries ago; we were not then born.

2. There is in Old-Testament history a second more serious difficulty, and that is the standing still

of the sun and moon at the command of Joshua to give him time to complete his victory. With our lack of knowledge we cannot declare this to be impossible. We were not there and cannot speak with authority. It may be that the language is figurative. We speak of the sun rising and setting, though it does neither. Or perhaps the words in Joshua are a poetic way of saying that it was a good day's work; what ordinarily would have required two days was accomplished in one by the help of Jehovah, who lengthened the day in results if not literally. This interpretation receives some sanction when we come to read the sacred record, and find that the words which give us trouble are a poetical quotation from what is termed "the book of Jasher." Joshua prayed for time thoroughly to conquer the enemy, and so favorable were the accompanying circumstances that the victory was complete before the sun went down. If now a poet, Jasher, chose to represent the sun as standing still, it was a beautiful thought, and naturally would be incorporated into the historical account of the battle. Homer makes Agamemnon to pray to Jove:

> "Let not the sun go down and night come on
> Ere I shall lay the halls of Priam waste."

That was poetry, which meant that he wanted victory that day. This is one explanation which really does away with the miracle, but most hold that there was a miraculous lengthening of the day for Joshua. It is not, however, very generally thought that the earth stopped in its revolution. If it did, the way in which the phenomenon would be described would be that the sun stood still, and not that the earth halted in its revolving, for we say the sun rises and sets, although strictly we ought to say the earth rolls round into the light and out of it again, making day and night. There is no difficulty, therefore, in the fact that the *sun* was said to stand still (it was using language popularly, just as we do), but the difficulty is, How could the earth have been arrested in its diurnal motion without throwing all off its surface, and without a shock to the whole solar system? Of course infinite Power could hold everything in its place, and could prevent any catastrophe, but it is more natural to suppose that the desired end was accomplished by less violent means. We are all acquainted with the laws of refraction. In the mirage, for instance, distant scenes ordinarily out of sight are lifted into view. How? There is a modification of the atmosphere, and the rays of light are so bent as to fall upon our vision even over an intervening obstacle. This is not theory, but an atmospherical fact which has been repeatedly observed. Now, what if the sun did actually set when Joshua was fighting his battle? The air may have been so changed that the rays were refracted over the hills between, so that the sun would seem

FORMIDABLE OBJECTIONS. 85

to be in the open sky. In that way could the day be lengthened. That there was such a day seems the more probable when we are told that there is a Chinese tradition of a day double the usual length. Then there is the familiar Greek fable, that the sun was once persuaded by a rash boy of his to let him drive the flaming chariot across the heavens, and the result was that the youth was run away with, and the fiery steeds rushed up and down the skies, not reaching the western gates till long after the usual time. That seems to be the mythological way of stating that there has been one day when the sun was later than usual in setting. Who, therefore, shall assert that the sun did not to all intents and purposes stand still for Joshua? We were not there, we were not born over three millenniums ago, and in our ignorance we will show some wisdom by not denying what both tradition and Scripture declare. At any rate, the strange phenomenon is capable of a poetical and even scientific explanation.

3. In passing let me merely allude to the much-discredited story of Jonah. Possibly, the narrative, if fictitious, could be used for the moral instruction conveyed by it in the Bible, for the Lord himself taught by parables, by stories; but we can scarcely resist the conviction that Christ refers to the experience of the prophet of Nineveh as historical, for Jonah and Solomon and the queen of the south are spoken of together. Besides, the great Teacher

makes the entombment in the sea-monster typical of his own three days spent in the grave; and the parallel is not very exact or impressive if both are not facts. We believe in the Lord's burial and resurrection, and this is the greater miracle of the two. Nor is the lesser miracle, to my mind, so very incredible. There are marine animals large enough to swallow a man. In the capacious stomach of a dog-fish a horse has been found whole, and likewise a warrior in full armor. These are not fictions. It is an authenticated case, that of the sailor who in 1758 was swallowed without mutilation by a leviathan of the deep. The only thing miraculous about the scriptural story is the preservation of the prophet alive under the circumstances. And why should this be regarded a thing incredible with God, who in the works of creation and in other recorded miracles that are generally accepted performs still greater wonders? If you impeach the testimony of God's word as to the sign of the prophet Jonah, there must at least be admitted the ironical truthfulness of the scriptural representation of such as you:

"Doubtless, thou knowest, for thou wast then born,
And the number of thy days is great!"

4. One more difficulty, and that is in relation to the Flood. There is the witticism about the ventilation of the ark with its one little window; but a scholar would never have made the egregious

blunder of supposing that there was only one small aperture for the admission of light and air. The Hebrew word implies that there was a system of windows, running, it would seem, just beneath the roof, the whole length of the ark, and when Noah opened the window for the raven and dove, a different word is used (as the Revised Version, though not the old, indicates), showing that this was a single compartment in the larger window or "light." Nor is the objection that the ark was not large enough for all the different animals of any force, when we understand that it is not necessary to suppose there was a universal deluge. To be sure, we read of "all flesh" being destroyed, of the waters covering "all the high mountains that were under the whole heaven," but we also read of a decree going out from Cæsar Augustus "that all the world should be enrolled" in the census of the first century. As the latter means simply the Roman empire, all the world in which Augustus had any interest, so the former may mean the world so far as Noah was concerned. Such general expressions need not be taken literally, any more than we are when we say, "Everybody is going to such and such a place." The ark, which was a little larger than the Great Eastern, may not have been capable of holding two of every species around the entire globe, but all the animals (two and two of them) of the land which we may suppose to have been swept by a partial flood may have had sufficient room. But is there any evidence (outside of the Bible) of even a local flood of any great extent? Yes; almost all nations have traditions of a destructive deluge. As the descendants of Noah multiplied and were dispersed over the earth, the memory of the great catastrophe would naturally be passed down the ages, although, of course, variations would arise. There is, accordingly, the account of Berosus, in many respects resembling the scriptural narrative. The Chinese have a story that all the world was once drowned except three emperors. The Greeks had their Deucalion, who built a ship in which he and his wife were saved from an inundation which destroyed all the rest of mankind. Among the American Indians are various traditions, one of which makes it the humming-bird that returns with a twig in its beak. Now, all this proves that there must have been some original fact which gave rise to the different stories. Nor is the deluge an unlikely event, looking at it from a geological standpoint. Only as long ago as "June, 1819," says the geologist Lyell, "the sea flowed in by the eastern mouth of the Indus, and in a few hours converted a tract of land two thousand square miles in area into an inland sea." We are familiar with geological elevations and depressions of land. Winchell, in his *Sketches of Creation*, says that "in 1822 the entire coast of Chili was elevated to a height varying from two to seven feet —an extent equal to the area of New England and New York having been lifted up bodily." The same geologist declares that "a depression in the valley of the Lower Mississippi of only three hundred feet would admit the waters of the Gulf of Mexico up to the mouth of the Ohio." When Dawson, even from the scientific standpoint, tells us of geological deluges submerging the plains of Europe under one thousand feet of water, and informs us that the earth since the advent of man has taken at least one such "plunge-bath before attaining its modern fixity," we need not be very skeptical about a Bible flood, partial or universal; we need not in the least discredit that of the time of Noah. God very properly says,

"Where wast thou when I laid the foundations of the earth?
Declare, if thou hast understanding.
  * * * * * *
Doubtless, thou knowest, for thou wast then born,
And the number of thy days is great!"

We were not present when the great deep in the time of Noah is said to have been broken up, and we have no right to deny what is written as fact, what is sustained by universal tradition and what is rendered probable by geologic science.

In conclusion, whether we believe in the deluge or not, there is coming the flood of death which will be to each of us a terrible reality. There is no getting around the waters of that Jordan, and unhappy shall we be if this mighty tide sweep us out into eternity while we are scoffing. We will then wish to be in one ark, and that is the ark of salvation. Seek safety in time, for there is such a thing as being too late.

"Come to the ark, ere yet the flood
Your lingering steps oppose;
Come, for the door which open stood
Is now about to close."

CHAPTER VII.

INCIDENTAL CONFIRMATIONS OF THE BIBLE.

"Behold, the ships also, though they are so great, and are driven by rough winds, are yet turned about by a very small rudder, whither the impulse of the steersman willeth."
—JAMES 3:4.

THE apostle is arguing against setting up to be "teachers" of divine things. He implies that special qualifications are required for the responsible position of making known the will of God. Self-constituted teachers are sure to make mistakes from which the inspired are free. "If any man," says the context, "stumbleth not in word, the same is a perfect man." "The tongue," James says, "is a little member," but it can easily make a slip. The truth of this we recognize in the oft-used Latin phrase, *lapsus linguæ*, a slip of the tongue. Now, the teachers whom God inspired to give us a perfect rule of faith and practice, to give us the Scriptures, have *not* stumbled even in word. A slight inaccuracy, a slip of the tongue as to any essential fact, would be an impeachment of the veracity of the Bible, but such we do not find. If we did, it would throw the Old and New Testaments out of the course of the divinely given, and would leave us all at sea religiously. On the other hand, a very trifling mark of truthfulness confirms our faith in the infallibility of Holy Writ, and the more indirect and casual the proof the stronger it is. Professor Blunt in his *Undesigned Coincidences,* and Paley in his *Horæ Paulinæ,* or *Hours with Paul,* have brought together a great many incidental confirmations of the Bible. A few of these, with others that have come to me in a personal investigation of the subject, will be passed before you for your consideration, and, it is to be hoped, for your edification.

The Scriptures of the Old and New Testaments have come down the ages like ships; they have been "driven by rough winds," they have been subjected to severe gales of criticism; but when they have seemed about to be lost on the rocks of skepticism and infidelity, they have been righted to their course by a subtle impulse given at the hand of the great Steersman. "Though they are so great," yet again and again they have been recovered to the faith of God's people by some undesigned agreement which has been made to appear between different ones of the sacred writers, by some unimportant allusion which has been found to be true to fact. Hence the significance of our text as applied to the Scriptures: "Behold, the ships also, though they are so great, and are driven by rough winds, are yet turned about by a very small rudder, whither the impulse of the steersman willeth." Undesigned coincidences will at this time be made repeatedly to be the very small rudder which God uses to bring back the Scriptures from where some would have them driven by contrary winds.

1. First, let us look at the Old Testament. When Joseph was sold by his brethren it was to a caravan, we read in Genesis, "bearing spicery, and balm and myrrh, going to carry it down to Egypt." There we see a mere allusion to a species of Oriental traffic carried on with the ancient Egyptians. There was no special occasion for mentioning the spicery that was being conveyed to Egypt; the sale of a brother was the main subject. But this small incident, to which only a passing reference is made, fits in with the fact that Egypt needed a great deal of this kind of merchandise, and that that country, therefore, was a probable and profitable market for balm from the East. Years afterward Joseph, as we are informed, "embalmed" his father, and it is implied that embalming was an Egyptian custom, while centuries subsequently we read in the Gospel of John about Nicodemus for the burial of Jesus "bringing a mixture of myrrh and aloes, about a hundred pound weight." If a hundred pounds were required for a single body, of course Egypt with its practice of embalming was a great market for spicery. So remarkably does an indirect allusion in Genesis tally with fact. The casual refer-

ence to spicery is the small rudder keeping the ship to the straight track of truthfulness.

Take, again, that great biblical event of the passage of the Jordan. When did it occur? According to the book of Joshua, it was (and it is stated parenthetically as being aside from the chief thing to be narrated) when "Jordan overfloweth all its banks all the time of harvest." The time is further indicated as being "on the tenth day of the first month." That we know from other sources to have been four days before the Passover. But the Israelites left *Egypt* at the Passover, just after the ten plagues, one of them being the hail by which it is said in Exodus "the *flax* and the barley were smitten." Now, three days before the crossing of the Jordan spies were sent into Jericho, where they were hidden by Rahab, and how? We read in Joshua that she "hid them with the stalks of *flax*, which she had laid in order upon the roof." The smiting of the flax with hail in one book corresponds with the hiding under flax in the other, and that, too, though neither writer was speaking of flax directly, but the one was describing a plague and the other the passage of the Jordan, both which events occurred at or near the Passover or harvest. They both happened, we say, to mention flax at its full development, and thus they unconsciously strengthen each other and our confidence in their veracity. They are mutually corroborative, and in the most incidental manner. The very indirectness of this kind of proof is what confirms our faith. It is the very small rudder which turns the whole ship, which recovers to our assured belief the whole Old Testament when driven by the rough winds of unbelief.

Again, we read in Numbers that the spies sent by Moses into Canaan saw "men of great stature," "sons of Anak." Joshua, however, it is said in the book bearing his name, "cut off the Anakim," "utterly destroyed them." But pass down to the time of David, and we learn from Samuel that the giants had *not* all been exterminated, for "Goliath of Gath" defied the armies of the living God. Turn back to Joshua, and see if they *did* entirely annihilate the Anakim, and see if you can account for "Goliath of Gath." Certainly you can, for just beyond what has already been quoted it is said, "There was none of the Anakim left in the land of the children of Israel: *only* in Gaza, in *Gath*, and in Ashdod, did some remain." Thus do we have three independent witnesses—Moses, Joshua and Samuel—agreeing, though they manifestly do not plan for the agreement. This is a little item to be taken into account in the consideration of so great a subject, but it is none the less important for that reason. A straw shows which way the wind blows. A very small rudder determines the course of a great ship. A very minor incident helps to establish the whole Old Testament in our convictions.

At the preaching of Jonah, to proceed in further illustration of our topic, there was such repentance that we read in the prophet there were "covered with sackcloth both man and *beast.*" A singular and an improbable way of mourning that was, to have the very beasts in the array of mourning. Is not the whole narrative of the preaching to the Ninevites proven a myth by this strange circumstance which is related as a fact? It might seem so until we take up a pagan writer, Plutarch, by whom we are informed that at the death of Pelopidas his soldiers "cut off their *horses'* manes and their own hair;" while at the death of a very dear friend Alexander the Great was so overcome "that to express his sorrow he immediately ordered the manes and tails of all his *horses and mules* to be cut." Thus does a pagan writer, without intending it, render credible the sacred writer, who says that the king of Nineveh, as an expression of repentance before God, ordered the very flocks and herds to be "covered with sackcloth." This is a little incident, but it confirms the truthfulness of Jonah, that most bitterly assailed of all the books of the Bible, and it thus assists in establishing the entire Old Testament. It is the very small rudder which turns the whole ship.

Another example: David in adversity experienced kindness from an aged Gileadite, and by way of reward he took into the royal favor a son of his friend by the name of "Chimham." There is only the barest allusion to it in Samuel and Kings. Exactly what David did for Chimham it is not said, but he probably gave him an estate in the vicinity of the court. The name, however, does not appear for four hundred years. May it not have been all a fable about Chimham experiencing the royal favor? Was it real history or was it a beautiful romance? We pass down four centuries and we find Jeremiah prophesying. He is describing a time of peril, and he is telling of some Jews trying to escape from the captivity which came, and he uses this language: "And they departed, and dwelt in Geruth (margin, the lodging-place of) *Chimham*, which is by Bethlehem, to go to enter into Egypt, because of the Chaldeans." Thus does it appear that Chimham was an actual person, that he really had experienced the royal favor by having an estate settled upon him—an estate which bore his name four hundred years after the event. What is more, the prophet was evidently not trying to confirm the earlier narrative, for the name of Chimham comes in only incidentally as a stopping-place for some Jewish refugees on the way to Egypt. So that by a dark hint to an event which transpired four centuries before, by a hint which not one reader in a thousand would notice, in so indirect a way is the word of God confirmed, and the confirmation is all the stronger because entirely undesigned.

Again, we read in Second Kings, "Now Mesha, king of Moab, was a sheepmaster; and he rendered unto the king of Israel the wool of an hundred thousand lambs, and of an hundred thousand rams." But this Moabite king rebelled; he determined to have relief from the oppressive tribute imposed. We learn further from the scriptural narrative that he was overwhelmingly defeated, but that he rallied in a last stronghold, and that there he made to his god, upon the wall in full sight of the besieging Israelites, the costly burnt-offering of his first-born son. And what was the result? The biblical answer is, "And there was great wrath against Israel: and they departed from him, and returned to their own land." That is, the Israelites, horrified at the human, and at the same time inhuman, sacrifice, relinquished the siege for fear of a divine judgment upon them as being indirectly the cause of the great wickedness committed, and the Moabite monarch thus gained his end, the independence of his kingdom, and, as he believed and as it seemed, through the divine favor secured by the open sacrifice of his son. This all seems very improbable, does it not? Happening, too, nine hundred years before Christ, it becomes the more doubtful, even if it is related in the Bible. But there has come in these recent times a remarkable confirmation of the scriptural story. In 1868 a traveler in the ancient territory of the Moabites came upon a stone three feet nine inches long, two feet four inches wide and one foot two inches thick. This is the famous Moabite Stone, one of the most marvelous discoveries in this century of wonders. It is now in Paris, and what does it contain? An inscription made by the Moabite king himself nine centuries before the Christian era, and establishing the truthfulness of the inspired record. "I, Mesha," is the reading in chiseled and imperishable characters, "erected this stone to Chemosh, . . . for he saved me from all despoilers and let me see my desire upon all my enemies." And who were among his enemies? The Moabite Stone replies, the "king of Israel, who oppressed Moab many days." Thus are the very stones crying out in defence of God's word and of our holy religion.

Still, again: profane historians relate that the capture of Babylon took place under Nabonnedus, not under Belshazzar, whom Daniel names.[6] Skeptics used to enlarge upon this discrepancy, as well as upon other contradictions. But a few years ago in the vicinity of Babylon was found a cylinder which gave the information that Nabonnedus had a son by the name of Belshazzar who was associated with the father in the government. A complete harmony is thus established between the profane historian and sacred narrator, while at the same time a casual remark of the latter is explained. Belshazzar, according to Daniel, had promised that the reader of the handwriting on the wall should be "*third* ruler in the kingdom." Why not second, instead of third? The association of two monarchs, Nabonnedus and Belshazzar, in ruling clears up what was long a mystery. The inspired writer casually remarks that the reader of the handwriting was to be made "third" in the kingdom, and no one knew why *third* till a cylinder a little while ago revealed the secret by its allusion to the Babylonian throne being occupied by father and son jointly, who of course would be first and second, although Daniel directly mentions only one of the two. We could go on indefinitely giving specifications of the incidental confirmation of the Old Testament. Repeatedly, a very small rudder rights in our faith the ship of God's word when driven by the rough winds of skeptical assault.

2. We have, in the second place, just as striking confirmations of the New Testament. Does Paul say in his Epistle to the Ephesians, "I am an ambassador in chains"? The historian in Acts makes him say, "I am bound with this chain." Does the historic narrative say, "Saul laid waste the Church"? He confirms this when he writes his letter to the Galatians, "Beyond measure I persecuted the Church of God." Does Luke write that Timothy was "the son of a Jewess"? Paul intimates (and an intimation is stronger proof sometimes than a direct assertion) the same thing when in his Epistle to Timothy he says, "From a babe thou hast known the sacred writings." To be sure, he had known the Scriptures from childhood if he had a Jewish mother. The words of Luke and Paul in this way, without design, are mutually

confirmatory. Does Luke affirm that the Sadducees say, "There is no resurrection, neither angel, nor spirit"? Josephus, who was born 37 A. D., and thus belonged to the first century of the Christian era, says, "The doctrine of the Sadducees is this, that souls die with the bodies." Thus Jew and Christian agree, and that, too, without collusion.

Quite aside from his main purpose, the writer of the Acts speaks of "the Beautiful Gate of the temple." The Jewish historian, without any reference to Luke, tells of a gate of the temple which "greatly excelled" the others, and which was "adorned after a most costly manner, as having much richer and thicker plates of silver and gold" than the rest. Did the priest of Jupiter, according to the Acts, bring "oxen and *garlands*" to sacrifice in honor of the apostles? In a triumph voted to an ancient general there figured, according to classic story (Plutarch), "a hundred and twenty stalled oxen, with their horns gilded and their heads adorned with ribbons and *garlands*." Thus accurate as to facts which we are inclined to dispute are the New-Testament writers, and when without contrivance they are corroborated by pagan testimony, we must believe that those who were faithful in recording what was least are equally trustworthy in their narration of weightier matters.

Did Paul slander the Cretans when in his letter to Titus he warned them against " teaching things which they ought not, for filthy lucre's sake"? Nay, this accords with the character ascribed to them by Plutarch in his life of Perseus, who was noted for being covetous, and who "cheated," it is said, his Cretan followers, not giving them the money he promised for some valuable plate. The historian adds, "He only played the Cretan with the Cretans." The inspired and the uninspired writers agree in the character ascribed to those islanders, and yet the harmony between the two was unintentional. A little and yet a significant circumstance is this: it is the very small rudder turning the whole ship, large though it be; it is one of those undesigned coincidences which confirm the truth of the whole New Testament.

Does this inspired book tell us of the crucifixion of Christ by Pilate, and of his followers being "called Christians"? The Roman Tacitus of the first century speaks of "persons commonly called Christians who were hated for their enormities. Christus, the founder of that name, was put to death as a criminal by Pontius Pilate." Does Luke in the Acts say, "Claudius had commanded all the Jews to depart from Rome"? Suetonius, a Latin contemporary, says of the same emperor, "He banished from Rome all the Jews, who were continually making disturbances at the instigation of one Chrestus;" that is, Christ. These are little things, but they harmonize wonderfully and without any purpose of that kind.

When the multitude was to be miraculously fed on the other side of the Sea of Galilee, John says that Jesus asked "Philip" where bread could be bought. Why, do you suppose, was the question directed to Philip? Well, we can ascertain why in a circuitous way. From Luke we learn that the exact locality of the miracle was in the vicinity of "a city called Bethsaida." Then we are told by John, but not in connection with the miracle, that "Philip was from Bethsaida." In this roundabout manner do we see why Philip was asked where bread could be secured. He was brought up in that neighborhood, and would know, if any one did, where the desired purchase could be made. This is indirect but very strong evidence for the truthfulness of John in that, without saying that the feeding of the multitude was at Bethsaida, he made Christ ask concerning a place for buying bread of the disciple who would be apt to know because of the locality being near his native city. It is one of those minor touches which establish the veracity of the New Testament.

Again does the small rudder appear when Paul in his letter to the Romans commends to them Phœbe, "a servant of the church which is at *Cenchrea*," and when it is remarked of him in the most casual way in the Acts, "having shorn his head in *Cenchrea*." The one reference shows that he was acquainted with a member of the church there, and the other that he had been there;

and without any intention they confirm each other and strengthen our faith in the whole New Testament.

Once more: we read in Colossians, "Onesimus, the faithful and beloved brother, *who is one of you;*" that is, one of the Colossians. Can this be, not directly, but indirectly, proved? Turn to Philemon, and Onesimus is found to be a "servant" of Philemon. But did Philemon live in Colosse? The letter to him does not give us any information on this point, but the Epistle *does* contain greetings to Philemon "*and* to *Archippus.*" Where did Archippus reside? The Epistle to the Colossians says, "Say to Archippus, Take heed to the ministry which thou hast received." So that Archippus was of Colosse, and hence Philemon was, who is coupled with him in the letter to Philemon, and therefore Onesimus was of Colosse, for he was a slave of Philemon; and in this circuitous manner is established the truth of what the apostle wrote to the Colossians: Onesimus, "*who is one of you.*" These circumstantial coincidences are what give credibility to the testimony of different witnesses in court, and it is these minute agreements without design which prove the truthfulness of the various writers of the New Testament.

The fact is, that both the Old Testament and the New are constantly being verified in the most indirect and yet positive ways by the marvelous discoveries which are taking place. There is the

INCIDENTAL CONFIRMATIONS. 105

oft-mentioned case, already referred to in a previous chapter, of the proper title of Sergius Paulus, who governed the island of Cyprus at the time of Paul's visit. Luke was long thought to have made a mistake in calling this ruler "proconsul" instead of "proprætor," but among the confirmations of his entire accuracy is none stronger than the finding by General Cesnola, in modern excavations at Cyprus, of a coin bearing the inscription, "*In the proconsulship of Paulus,*" who may have been the Sergius Paulus named by the sacred historian, and whose title at least was definitely fixed beyond all controversy. Two other very striking incidents are worth mentioning because of their important bearing. Since we read in Haggai, "and will make thee as a signet," very significantly, within a few years, at the sinking of a shaft to the depth of twenty-two feet at the city of Jerusalem, there has been discovered amid fragments of pottery and glass a gentleman's seal, a finely-grained black stone, with the inscription, "*Haggai the son of Shebaniah.*" The lettering is of the kind used at the time of the Babylonian Captivity. The prophet Haggai was one of the exiles who returned to Jerusalem under the lead of Zerubbabel. The seal found may therefore be the one which suggested Haggai's words when he said of his leader, "and will make thee as a signet." The prophet may have held up before Zerubbabel his own signet, and possibly the very seal lately exhumed, and certainly inscribed with the name of "*Haggai*."[7] When, again, like that noble Roman who bought at its full price the very ground on which the army of Hannibal was encamped, Jeremiah with all confidence in the future made his ancestral purchase in his native Anathoth over which the Babylonian engines of war were rolling, the prophet said of this famous business transaction, "I subscribed the deed, and sealed it." And how he prized his seal is indicated by that other verse in his prophecy where he represents God as saying of the king of Judah that though he "were the signet upon my right hand, yet would I pluck thee thence." In connection with all this is the very suggestive fact that among recent discoveries in Egypt, where we find the prophet in his later life, is a remarkable seal with Phœnician characters which read, "*To the Prosperity of Jeremiah.*" The type of lettering is assigned to the seventh century before Christ, and hence the seal, it has been said, "may be a veritable relic of the great Hebrew prophet Jeremiah." These surely are wonderful incidental confirmations of the prophetic writings.

The conclusion of the whole matter is, that both Testaments, Old and New, have come down many centuries over a tempestuous sea, assailed by fierce gales of an unbelieving criticism, but as often as they have been driven out toward the rocks of infidelity, they have been veered back into the confidence of Christians by some undesigned coincidence, by some incidental confirmation of their entire truthfulness. "Behold, the ships also, though they are so great, and are driven by rough winds, are yet turned about by a very small rudder, whither the impulse of the steersman willeth." So it has been with the Holy Scriptures, and let us thank God for their preservation and complete establishment in ways so circuitous and undesigned. God by a very small rudder has repeatedly kept them straight on their course to carry the gospel of glad tidings to all the world.

CHAPTER VIII.

THE BIBLE AND SCIENCE; OR, THE CREATIVE WEEK.

"For in six days the Lord made heaven and earth, the sea, and all that in them is, and rested the seventh day."— Ex. 20: 11.

WE will take a general and a specific view of the subject suggested by this text, which brings at once to our thought the topic of the Bible and Science.

1. The creative week, as described by Moses in the first chapter of Genesis, has probably caused more discussion than any other portion of Scripture; nor have Genesis and geology yet been harmonized in a way that satisfies all minds. There are those to whom the differences between religion and science at this very starting-point of the controversy seem irreconcilable, and they accordingly reject the whole scheme of revelation, and they acknowledge nothing but nature. The first article of the unbeliever's creed has been stated in this fashion: "I believe that there is no God, but that matter is God, and God is matter; and that it is no matter whether there is any God or not."

But while some consider the Mosaic cosmogony as wholly mythical, and while others regard it as allegorical—a picture at best of the great epochs in creation—most biblical scholars hold that the narrative is essentially historical and altogether true. Still, no intelligent interpreter now maintains that the whole creation took place in six literal days. That was for centuries the prevailing view (although Augustine and others of the early Fathers did not hold to it), but it was long the general view, which at first was not abandoned, though it *did* seem to conflict with geologic facts.

What if the sedimentary formations were such as to indicate a work of thousands and perhaps millions of years? It was argued that God *could* have formed the deposits at once. So could he form the blade of grass in an instant, but we see that he does not, and it is difficult to believe that he in a moment's time created the sandstones, whose formation a natural and protracted growth, such as is going on to-day, better explains. What if the rocks did contain fossil remains which seemed to show that animals and plants existed long ages before the assumed time of the creation? God could have instantly created a fossil, it was claimed, to represent an animal or a plant which never really existed. He perhaps could have done so, but it is not at all likely that he did.

That argument failed to satisfy the human mind. If, in excavating, the remains of a buried city should be exhumed, people *would* believe that it had been built there naturally by a generation of living men. Of course God *might* have imbedded in the earth, by a fiat of his, just such ruins when he called this universe into being, but only the most ignorant would give credence to any such theory. So the discovery of fossils deep down in sedimentary rocks which could have been formed by the slow deposits of waters only during a period far longer than the commonly accepted age of this world, forces the reason to believe that, for instance, the foot-tracks of those immense animals "which stalked on the Permian sands and mud" were impressed there naturally by those gigantic creatures when those alluvial deposits were made thousands and thousands of years ago, and that God *did not* six millenniums ago by a miraculous act imprint life-like tracks in the stratified layers just to deceive man. Likewise the petrified leaf or tree cannot be thought to be a supernatural, but a natural, formation. We did not *see* it turn to stone, but we know it did, because we can trace the original vegetable lines and characteristics. So that a *progressive* creation is no longer doubted, the progress extending over more than six days of twenty-four hours each.

There are two main methods of giving time for the geologic formations. The one is to fix a great gulf between the first verse of the inspired record and what follows: "In the beginning God created the heaven and the earth." To that indefinite period, "in the beginning," can be assigned those long ages of which we read in the books—Cambrian, Silurian, Carboniferous, or Primary, Secondary and Tertiary, or Azoic, Mesozoic and Palæozoic, and so on up through the technical list;—*these* all would belong to the "in the beginning." Then would follow six natural days, during which the previous chaotic disorder, by fiats of the Almighty, would be resolved into the beautiful cosmos which became the habitation of man.

The other method of reconciling the geologic and Mosaic records is to make the days to be vast stretches of time. The most prominent advocates of this view from the scientific standpoint are Professor Dana of Yale and the late Professor Guyot of Princeton College, and their explanations are certainly very plausible; and it is not strange that a large portion of Christendom seems to be settling down to an acceptance of the harmony which can thus be established. It violates no law of hermeneutics, no sound exegetical principle, to prolong indefinitely the six days of creation. We are assured by the sacred writers themselves that one day is with the Lord as a thousand years. Then such expressions as these are found in the Bible: "the day of salvation," "the day of wrath," "the day of temptation," "the day of trouble," "the day of Egypt," where manifestly there is no hour-limit. In the very narrative of the creation the word is employed to mark varying periods of duration. It occurs three times before the appearance of the sun at all — of that orb which gave the present succession of darkness and light. Once it is used to cover the whole process of the creation — "in the *day* that the Lord God made the earth and the heavens," this day being thus coextensive with the six days previously mentioned. As a matter of interpretation, therefore, there can be no objection to making the days denote geologic ages, as the scholarly Tayler Lewis long ago did in his famous *Six Days of Creation.*

A more important question is, Is the *order* of creation the same scripturally that it is scientifically? The parallelism is so marked as to have convinced the master-minds of even the eminent scientists to whom reference has been made that the two revelations, in the word of truth and in the work of nature, must be alike from God. The Yale professor, in his *Manual of Geology,* says: "The order of events in the Scripture cosmogony corresponds essentially with that which has been given" (in his book); and he sees in this "a far-reaching prophecy to which philosophy could not have attained, however instructed." The distinguished Princeton naturalist was so struck with the resemblances that he wrote a little volume on *Creation; or, The Biblical Cosmogony in the Light of Modern Science,* in which his enthusiasm kindles because of what he calls "the grand cosmogonic week described by Moses."

THE BIBLE AND SCIENCE. 113

Principal Dawson of Canada, in his *Origin of the World*, still more minutely presents the wonderful agreement of the Bible and science. It is the thoughts of such specialists that we have endeavored to assimilate and are trying to unfold.

In these times of skeptical contrasts drawn between creation and evolution, to the disparagement of the former, we need to bear in mind that they are not necessarily antagonistic—that there are theistic and Christian evolutionists, like the late Professor Gray of Harvard and botany fame, and like the lamented Agassiz.[8] Let us only become acquainted with the facts, and we shall not be frightened at infidel claims of divergence and opposition, and our faith will not waver in the least as we repeat the words spoken of old by inspiration : " For in six days the Lord made heaven and earth, the sea, and all that in them is, and rested the seventh day."

2. Turning now to details, let us follow along the latest paths of science over the creative week, and let us see how they do not diverge at all from the old paths of religion.

The first day, or geologic age, was characterized by the creation of matter and by the appearance of light. The universe was called into being, but in a chaotic or nebulous condition—" the earth was waste and void." A nebula was created, diffused through space, but this vapory mass was inert till God said, " Let there be light." This was not the light of the sun (which had not yet appeared), but cosmical

8

light, a light produced by molecular action. The Almighty imparted a rotary motion to the igneous mass; he set it revolving; he gave it laws of action which still operate in gravity, in chemical and other natural forces. This was the beginning, a fire-mist turning on an axis, matter in activity. "A flash of light through the universe," says the scientist (Dana condensing from Guyot), "would be the first announcement of the work begun." So much for the first day, for its evening and morning—"a familiar metaphor," we are told (Dana) with apparent good reason, to indicate "the beginning and consummation of each work," for there was as yet no solar day. There was simply luminosity from the movements of multitudinous atoms.

The second day, or geologic age, was marked by the separation of the waters from the waters by a firmament. The gaseous would in time by contraction become the molten, of the consistency of water. Such waters were separated from waters; the great watery bulk broke up into different globules of still immense proportions. On the first day matter was created and endowed with force, but it was *one* whirling, fluid mass, with vast sphericity. As it cooled and condensed it would revolve more and more rapidly, till the centrifugal force became greater than the centripetal, and portion after portion, like so many watery drops, would be thrown off, each assuming a spheroidal shape by the laws of motion. One of these vast revolving masses would be the original material of our solar system, which in turn would break up, and the planets would in this way be formed; and they too, as often as they threw off a portion of their still liquid bulk, would have a satellite or moon. Thus our present solar system would be gradually produced or evolved, with the central mass constituting the sun, which is still a glowing, heated ball. This dividing and subdividing of primordial matter occupied the second day. The earth, before included in the general mass, was individualized, was given a separate existence, a definite shape. Its waters were divided off from the other waters. This liquid globe of ours became defined, disentangled from the rest of the fire-mist. The exact words of the scientist (Guyot) in describing the work of the second day are: "The vast primitive nebula of the first day breaks up into a multitude of gaseous masses, and these are concentrated into stars." One of these nebulous stars would be the earth.

The third day came, and with it, according to the biblical narrative, continents and oceans and vegetation. This accords with the geological facts. The unfinished earth would cool and contract, and the condensed vapors would make a sea covering the entire surface of the globe. The heated sphere with its cooling crust would naturally crumple up, form into great wrinkles, acquire elevations and depressions, and there would thus result the sea and the dry land. Then the lower plant-organisms would start, while yet the waters were too hot for animal life; and it is worth observing that some forms of vegetation can exist at two hundred degrees Fahrenheit. The earth would be a great humid, shaded hothouse, giving rise to those luxuriant growths to which the everlasting rocks testify, when ferns attained the height of our most stately forest trees. Whether vegetation developed without a creative act from existent matter is not clear. One thing is certain, no experiments have yet succeeded in arranging material particles so as to produce living species; spontaneous generation is yet unproved. Possibly vegetation did develop from matter endowed from the beginning with germinant force under favorable conditions, for the language is, "Let the earth *bring forth.*" There was an absolute creation on the first day, but the word "create" is not used of the work of the second day, when, therefore, the earth may have been, and seems to have been, *evolved* from the general mass; and the word "create" is not used of the work of the third day, when it would seem as if continents and oceans were formed by a natural process, and when possibly vegetation was developed from the earth, and not strictly created; when the creation would be mediate —from pre-existent materials. These are unsettled points, but there is no doubt as to the agreement in the main events of the third day in Genesis and of the corresponding age in geology.

Strange as it may seem, Moses has no sun, no

moon, no stars till the fourth day; but this, too, is in accordance with the revelation which science has to make. While the earth was hot it would have a steaming atmosphere. Thick vapors would constantly rise from the waters, and there would never be the absence of dense clouds. Even when the first vegetation appeared at a possible temperature of two hundred degrees, there must have arisen great volumes of steam. The humidity of the air must have been beyond anything experienced now, even in our fogs that fairly drip and that prevent vision farther than a few feet. By continued cooling the water would to a less and less degree be converted into cloud, and the encircling envelope of fog would at length break and vanish, and the sun would for the first time blaze forth. The moon would also swing in her orbit a thing of beauty, and the stars would flash their brightness on the scene. Thus "God made two great lights" on the fourth day, so we read, "and he made the stars also." That is, he made them to *appear*, for the word here is not "create." What wonderful exactness of language! and how amazing that the unscientific Moses had our luminaries to shine forth in just the right geologic time! He had them *created* in the beginning, when they belonged to the first nebulous mass, but he did not have them outlined in a clear sky till the earth had sufficiently cooled to cease forming impenetrable clouds. Verily, great and marvelous are God's works as they appear in the scriptural and scientific facts connected with the fourth day in the creative week.

The fifth day consistently introduces the lower orders of animal life, which yet is higher than vegetable life, and here for the first since the original creation the strong word "create" occurs, as if to teach that there is no development from plant to beast.

The sixth day ushers in the higher animals, with man to crown the work, and with reference to him again a *creation* is asserted, and repeated three times, as if to emphasize his entire distinctness from the brute, out of which he could not have been evolved any more than the animal from the plant; and the scientist himself (Dana) bears this testimony: "No remains of ancient man have been found that are of a lower grade than the lowest of existing tribes; none that show any less of the erect posture and of other characteristics of the exalted species." Of the development of animal life from its lowest forms up through the reptilian age, when great bird-like and kangaroo-shaped creatures raising themselves on their hind legs stood eighty feet high in our own Colorado—of the progress of animal life up to man during the fifth and sixth days—Guyot says that Scripture gives "the precise order indicated by geology."

Thus the harmony between the six days of Genesis and the corresponding ages of geology is complete. Both recognize a gradual development, and both find crises where evolution must be supplemented by creation; and the only question of debate is how often the purely creative acts occurred. An *original* creation can never be disproved, and if it should be finally established that humanity itself was evolved out of some primordial organism, there will still be a Creator to adore and worship in Him who could endow a floating nebula with such potency as to develop a system of worlds, a fiery globe, a green earth, bright skies, bird and beast, and that lord of all—imperial man.

The seventh day well came with its absence of special creative energy, extending over the entire history of mankind. The era of human existence is God's Sabbath. It also is a *geologic* day, having lasted already at least six thousand years, during which God has, in a measure, been resting. Such is the creative week, with its culminating glory in this wonderful Sabbatic age of man. And Guyot notes a striking circumstance when he says, "At the end of each of the six working days of creation we find an evening. But the morning of the seventh is not followed by any evening. The day is still open. When the evening shall come the last hour of humanity will strike." As this moment, practically for each of us, is rapidly approaching in the certainty of death, and as God has his Sabbath of holy complacency in his work, let us, in our smaller way, after our six days of labor have a seventh when we can be still and worshipful, when we can contemplate such noble themes as that which has been occupying our attention. May we ever after this, in view of the thought which has been presented, be able to say with a sublimer significance, with a firmer faith, with a more devotional and reverent spirit, and with a gladder heart, "Remember the Sabbath day, to keep it holy. . . . For in six days the Lord made heaven and earth, the sea, and all that in them is, and rested the seventh day."

CHAPTER IX.

THE BIBLE AND THE MUMMIES OF THE PHARAOHS.

"And shewedst signs and wonders upon Pharaoh, and on all his servants, and on all the people of his land; for thou knewest that they dealt proudly against them; and didst get thee a name, as it is this day."—NEH. 9:10.

IN the spring of 1887 the papers contained the startling news that the remains of Lincoln had been examined and recognized preparatory to what might be hoped to be the final interment of our great martyr-President. More than twenty years had elapsed since he died, but his features still bore the old familiar expression. Wonderful, we say, that the loved face of the distinguished dead should have been kept in such a state of preservation! More marvelous is the fact to which our attention is now to be directed. Through the eyes of actual observers we are to look upon the countenances of some of the Pharaohs of Egypt. Napoleon stimulated his soldiers to gain the celebrated victory at the battle of the Pyramids as in full view of those monuments of antiquity he said, "From those summits forty centuries contemplate your actions." To-day not only the stupendous works of the Pharaohs, but those monarchs themselves, are literally looking down upon all travelers to Egypt in the mummies which have lately been discovered at Thebes.

Many have been growing incredulous of what is related in the Bible of the ancient rulers of Egypt in connection with biblical characters. Skepticism has been assailing Moses, has been sneering at his "mistakes," till some have come to regard him as a mythical personage. The story of Joseph has been called a beautiful romance, but nothing more. One school of the higher criticism has been trying to undermine the historical accuracy of the whole Pentateuch. "The signs and wonders upon Pharaoh" of which the text speaks have been regarded as idle tales, as the imaginations of superstitious minds, like the fables with which classic story abounds. But just when the assaults of infidelity upon the early scriptural narratives have been made with the greatest confidence of utterly demolishing the foundations of revealed religion, there have come confirmations of the Bible truly astonishing. Greater, if anything, than the miracles of old have been the revelations of the last few years, whereby the mummies of some of the greatest of the Pharaohs have been discovered.

It is well known that embalming was carried to a state of almost perfection by the Egyptians. For centuries the art was practiced, and it has been estimated that there must be in the land of the

THE BIBLE AND THE PHARAOHS. 123

Nile from four hundred to seven hundred million mummies. These are constantly being brought to light, and a few dollars will now purchase one of these dry, shriveled bodies of ages ago.

In 1881 there flashed over the wires to England, France and the whole world the announcement of a rich "find" of royal mummies. In 1882 came the official reports of professors and archæological authorities. Experts in Egyptology had for some time been struck with rare ornaments coming into circulation, the inscriptions on which indicated that they had been worn by royalty in very remote times. These came from three brothers who would not reveal the source whence they were deriving a very handsome revenue. They hinted that they had greater treasures yet which might in the future be produced for a consideration. They, however, kept their profitable secret till the imprisonment of one of them, and the fear of the other two that he would divulge the secret and alone receive the promised reward, led to the revealing of the place—a cave full of royal mummies.

In the solid rock anciently had been sunk a shaft six feet and a half square and about thirty-seven feet deep. At the bottom of this was a long and winding passage, ending in a chamber or vault twenty-three feet long by thirteen feet wide. In this subterranean room reposed nearly forty mummies, some of which have proved to be the embalmed bodies of the greatest of the Pharaohs.

They were removed, and packed as so much freight in a modern steamer, which, puffing and whistling, bore them triumphantly over the very waters along which had swept the magnificent funeral-barges of the same mighty dead between three and four thousand years ago. What a commentary on human greatness! Those mummied Pharaohs now adorn a museum at Boolak on the Nile, a short distance from Cairo. These are the "signs and wonders upon Pharaoh," to quote from our text, "as it is this day."

What Pharaohs have been found? Pharaoh was the name of an office rather than of any one ruler. It was like Cæsar in Roman annals, like Czar in Russian history, like President in our own country. It meant "Great House," and thus corresponded to "Sublime Porte" in Turkey at present. The house of Pharaoh *was* great. It furnished a long line of famous monarchs who reigned in splendor through hundreds of years. They dealt proudly against God's people, but Nehemiah declares that the Lord got him a name by the "signs and wonders upon Pharaoh." This was true of the miracles wrought anciently, and it is no less true of the mummies which have been providentially found just when the attacks upon the Mosaic books have been most severe and confident. The higher criticism of the skeptical sort goes down before the mummied Pharaohs who have been authenticated, duly numbered and laid away on shelves. Let us inquire who some of them are.

THE BIBLE AND THE PHARAOHS. 125

1. It is not certain who the Pharaoh of Joseph's time was, but among those unwrapt in the summer of 1886 was Thotmes the Third, who is noted as the great obelisk-maker, and Joseph lived in On, the city of the Sun, where the obelisks principally stood. They were meant to point to the orb of day, that object of Egyptian worship, somewhat as our church-spires point heavenward to direct our thoughts thither. When the sarcophagus of Thotmes, the obelisk-maker, was opened, there was discovered a little wasp which had evidently been attracted by the perfumes and the flowers used in burial, and which had inadvertently been sealed up with the dead monarch. Thotmes was not tall, only five feet and two inches, but he seems to have had lofty aspirations, or he would not have erected so many obelisks, one of which now stands in Central Park, New York City. That is something very tangible to link us to the distant past. There is nothing mythical and unreal about that grand pyramid of stone, weighing over two hundred tons, but slender and graceful, and tapering needle-like to a point, so that when Augustus Cæsar had it removed to Alexandria to commemorate his conquest of Egypt soon after the death of the most beautiful of Egyptian queens, it was not inappropriately called Cleopatra's Needle—a name which it still bears, although it was first erected by Thotmes in the city of Joseph's residence. There it stood, with others, at the entrance to the temple of the Sun. It is not

certain when Joseph lived, but if at the later date to which he is assigned by scholars, then he looked upon this identical obelisk. His father-in-law, the priest of On, daily passed it as he went into the temple to officiate at the altar. This priest's daughter, who became the wife of Joseph, in this case, must have often been helped in her devotions by the stately monolith reaching with its top toward the sky, the source of light. As another has said, the morning she became a bride would be ushered in by prayers whose inspiration would in part arise from the sight of the heavenward-pointing obelisk upon which we to-day gaze with awe and pleasure, and at whose base the traveler stands amid a rush of historic memories. Whether Joseph and his Egyptian wife saw this obelisk or not—they probably did not—they at any rate saw that father of obelisks which still stands at Heliopolis, and which, we are told, was raised on its pedestal before Abraham was born. Now the great obelisk-maker was Thotmes, whose mummy, with others, has recently been unrolled. Unfortunately, he crumbled to dust soon after his exposure to the air, but not till he had been photographed. We can therefore look upon the picture of the Pharaoh who did most to adorn with obelisks the city where Joseph rose to distinction. How much more real such a fact makes the person with whose dramatic history we are familiar as from slavery and the dungeon he rose to be second only to Pharaoh!

The Pharaoh who did most for the city where Joseph married his wife has been seen within the last three years. His mummied face has been actually observed by more than one, and a granite column which he made can be seen by every visitor to the metropolis of our country. How strange and wonderful it all is! "Signs and wonders upon Pharaoh" "as it is this day."

2. Another Pharaoh whose mummy in the Boolak Museum is putting honor upon God's word is Seti the First. We read in Scripture of "Pharaoh's daughter" who went down to the river to bathe, and who saw caught in reeds of the Nile a beautiful babe in a little ark. We have always had a warm feeling for the princess who was touched by the tears of the helpless innocent, and who named him Moses, which means "drawn out," in allusion to his having been taken out of the water. How we would like to look upon the kindly face of her to whom the young sister of the saved child went with a proposition to find a nurse, while the ingenious plan was carried out of the mother herself being brought for the tender service! How we would like to see the features of Pharaoh's daughter, who gave Moses his early training, initiating him into "all the wisdom of the Egyptians"! We may yet see the face of this fair princess. Meanwhile we are permitted to look upon the face of her supposed father (or possibly grandfather), Seti, who may have begun the Oppression, but who now lies a mummy in

a museum on the Nile not far from the place where the child Moses was rescued from a fate which actually was that of multitudes of other babes. Great power had this Pharaoh then, but now his sarcophagus is in an English museum, and he himself is fated to serve as a curiosity on the very scene of his tyranny. He graces a niche at Boolak, and of him Dr. C. S. Robinson says, with a fine sarcasm, "the most beautiful mummy-head which ever found a place in the museum." Such is the father, as is believed, of "Pharaoh's daughter." Can it be possible? It is, wonderfully confirming the word of God. It is among the "signs and wonders upon Pharaoh" "as it is this day."

3. The next Pharaoh has been identified beyond all shadow of a doubt as the one who specially made the Israelites to sigh and groan "by reason of the bondage." In Exodus we read of the poor slaves, "And they built for Pharaoh store-cities, Pithom and Raamses." Recent excavations have laid bare one of these, Pithom. What is seen? A brick wall twenty-two feet thick and six hundred and fifty feet along each side. Nearly all the enclosed space is occupied with solidly-built square chambers, separated by brick walls eight to ten feet thick, without windows or doors. This, from the inscriptions, has been found to be Pithom, and Rawlinson, the historian and Egyptologist, says there is "no reasonable doubt that one of the two cities built by the Israelites has been laid bare." It

is also stated that some of the bricks are of a superior and others of an inferior quality, some with straw and others without, or at least without the proper quality and quantity. It was bricks for this store-city that the Israelites had to furnish in undiminished numbers each day, even after government had ceased to provide straw, and they had to "find it" as best they could, while they succeeded in getting only "stubble for straw." What a confirmation there is here of the truth of the Mosaic record!

The other store-city, Raamses, has not yet been discovered, but a statue of its builder has been found. It is a colossal figure weighing four hundred tons, having been cut from a single block of stone. This bears upon its girdle the name of Rameses the Second (or Great). Fragments of another still larger statue of this monarch have been found here and there, and we are informed that if the scattered pieces were put together they would make an image ninety feet high, with a weight of nine hundred tons. On so large a scale did Rameses build, and he built by his Hebrew slaves Pithom which has actually been unearthed, and Raamses, bearing his name and likely yet to be brought to light.

But why speak of his statues and monuments when we have the king himself? Among the mummies lately unrolled was that of the Pharaoh who knew not Joseph. Rameses, the Pharaoh of the Oppression, adorns the museum at Boolak. His funeral regalia, the cerements of death, the successive bandages were removed in the presence of a distinguished company of Egyptians, Turks, Englishmen and representatives of other nations. Amid breathless attention the old tyrant was unwrapt, and, entirely stripped, the great oppressor of the Israelites lay before those at whose mercy he was more completely even than were at his mercy the Hebrews whose lives he made so bitter in the brickyards. We feel the reality of the oppression which drove the Israelites into rebellion when we can look upon the great oppressor himself. It gives us solid satisfaction to see his poor mummy examined to-day as a curiosity.

We can look without a fear upon his forehead, described as "low and narrow;" his eyebrows, "thick and white;" his small eyes; his aquiline nose; his ears, pierced for the wearing of jewelry; his broad shoulders; and his tall frame, over six feet in height. We can go to Egypt and see all this—gaze upon the great Rameses. Or if we cannot take the trip to the distant land of the Nile, we can at least get a photograph of this ancient monarch. Our very newspapers contain cuts of his mummied head and shoulders. Let some modern brickmaker adopt his face as a trade-mark to be stamped upon the plastic clay, and the revenges of time, or rather of Divine Providence, will be complete. The mummied remains of the oppressor,

Rameses, are among the "signs and wonders upon Pharaoh" "as it is this day." These are no ancient, but they are modern, Egyptian miracles almost. The truth in the case of the Pharaohs of the Bible is stranger than fiction.

4. The Pharaoh of the Exodus itself has not yet been found. We know who he was. He was a son of Rameses, and was called Menephtah the First. Very significantly, a monument of his in the Berlin Museum speaks of the sudden and melancholy death of a son of his. Could this calamity have occurred when every house in Egypt mourned its first-born except where the blood was sprinkled on the doorposts?

Is it all a myth about the ten plagues? Herodotus even speaks of a judgment visited upon Menephtah. Says the father of historians of this monarch: "He impiously hurled a spear into the overflowing waves of the river, which a sudden wind caused to rise to an unusual height;" and for this defiance of Deity he was smitten with a ten years' blindness. So that, according to this pagan writer, there was at least one plague inflicted upon this Pharaoh; and indeed the plagues were ten if the number of years be taken into account. From this Greek source he is seen to have had just the spirit, proud and imperious, which the Pharaoh of the Exodus had.

But where is his mummy to confirm the Bible story regarding his career? It has not yet been found, and perhaps never will be, for all his host was overthrown in the Red Sea, and he himself may also have perished thus, for "there remained not so much as one of them," and the Psalmist says God "overthrew Pharaoh *and* his host in the Red Sea." To be sure, his body may have been recovered and embalmed, and perhaps, as some biblical scholars maintain, he himself was not drowned at all, the scriptural expression being simply one of the common universals; but it is at least significant that though we have the mummy of his father and grandfather, his is missing. His unembalmed body may be lying at the bottom of the Red Sea. The very absence, therefore, of the mummy of the Pharaoh of the Exodus is confirmatory of God's word. His absence from the museum on the banks of the Nile is as significant as the presence of others. "Signs and wonders upon Pharaoh" "as it is this day"! That vacant niche at Boolak is a sign and wonder.

5. Among the most natural of mummied faces lately brought to light is that of Pinotem the Second, whose portrait appears in *Harper's Monthly* for July, 1882. The mummies of his wife and infant child are also among the recent discoveries. The babe, only sixteen inches long and reposing in the same sarcophagus as the queen, tells the sad story of their deaths, perhaps three thousand years ago. The little one barely saw the light of earth, and then lay down with the mother in the long

sleep of death. There is pathos in such revelations.

Now, some scholars identify Pinotem with the Pharaoh whose daughter Solomon married. If this be correct, we may say with the honorary secretary of the Egypt Exploration Fund (Amelia B. Edwards), and therefore eminent authority, "It is surely a strange subject for reflection that while Solomon and all his glories have passed away, the father, mother and infant sister of his Egyptian bride may be seen to this day under a glass case in the Boolak Museum." This is only re-echoing Scripture: "signs and wonders upon Pharaoh" "as it is this day."

Finally, what further signs and wonders God has in store for the strengthening of our faith we do not know. Jacob was "embalmed" in Egypt, and he was laid away in the cave of Machpelah. Not since the Mohammedan possession of this sacred place nor within the memory of man has any one been admitted to the innermost part of the cave. If entrance ever should be gained thereto in the innermost shrine, said Dean Stanley, "one at least of the patriarchal family may possibly still repose intact—the embalmed body of Jacob."

So, too, the "bones" of Joseph, which were so carefully preserved in Egypt during the long sojourn of his descendants there—those bones concerning which he gave commandment at his death that at the departure of the Israelites for the promised land they should be taken along—those bones which were carried up and down for forty years in the wilderness, and which were subsequently interred by Joshua at Shechem, to be transferred, possibly at a later date, according to the Mussulman tradition, to the cave of Machpelah,—those "bones" of Joseph, his embalmed body, may yet be found. Just as strange things have happened in the discovery of the mummy of the Pharaoh who "knew not Joseph."

But signs and wonders enough we have had to make us see the truth of religion and of the Bible, and to make us realize the vanity of all that is earthly. Of the four to seven hundred million mummies reposing in the sandy soil of Egypt, we have been looking at only a few; but surely these have been sufficient to impress us with the thought of human mortality. Soon we all shall be sleeping in the dust of the earth, and centuries hence our bones may be lying in museums. The "signs and wonders upon Pharaoh" "as it is this day" should teach us the solemn lesson of the frailty of our bodies, and should lead us to give due attention to the immortal part. During the thirty to forty centuries through which the mummies of the Pharaohs have come down to us,—during this long sleep of physical death the Pharaohs themselves, their immortal spirits, have been living somewhere. When not forty but a thousand and a million centuries of eternity have rolled away, our souls will still be in existence. How impressive the fact of such a sweep of centuries! Let us prepare for the endless future, for God will get him a name upon all who are enemies to spiritual Israel, and who deal proudly against the Church of Christ founded on apostles and prophets.

CHAPTER X.

ELEVATING INFLUENCE OF THE BIBLE.

"Thy word is a lamp unto my feet,
And light unto my path.—Ps. 119 : 105.

WHEREVER the Bible goes it dissipates darkness. Its elevating influence is unquestioned. Let a traveler in a wild, forsaken country put up for the night in an out-of-the-way, suspicious-looking house, and he might feel uneasy about his life and money. But let the good old Book be taken down, and let the head of the family reverently read therefrom in evening worship, and one would fear no longer; he would go to his rest with a feeling of perfect safety. An anecdote is related of some skeptical sailors, of their being wrecked on an isle of the sea, and of how they were afraid of being eaten by cannibals till some of them, creeping cautiously from the shore to the top of a hill, saw in the valley below the spire of a Christian church, whereupon they leaped to their feet, and called to their fellows that it was all right. Why that sudden sense of security? Because even those infidels knew that where the Bible and the church were, manners would be humanized. These are practical tests to show the real divineness of the Scriptures. Now let us note the elevating influence of the Bible along certain great lines.

1. Not to discuss the gradual undermining of slavery since the introduction of New-Testament ideas of brotherhood, till, instead of two bondmen to one freeman throughout the Roman empire at the advent of Christ, human bondage is now practically extinct throughout Christendom,—with this barest allusion, passing over a recognized reformation that has been wrought by scriptural teaching along the line of individual liberty, mark the change that has taken place with reference to childhood. Every reader of classical literature is acquainted with the ancient practice of exposing infants. Paris, who abducted the beautiful Helen and thus brought on the Trojan war, was in infancy abandoned on Mount Ida. Romulus and Remus, the founders of the Eternal City, were, according to the traditional story, thrown into the Tiber. Plato, in stating his doctrine of the community of families, says: "Their children are also common, and no parent is to know his child nor any child his parent." And what was to be the disposition of the little ones in the ideal republic? Why, this: "The proper officers will take the offspring of the good parents to the pen or fold, and there they will deposit them with certain nurses who dwell in a separate quarter; but the offspring of the inferior, or of the better when they chance to be deformed,

they will conceal in some mysterious, unknown place. Decency will be respected." That is from Plato, whom Joseph Cook places among the celestials. Then nursing-mothers were to be taken to the fold under such precautions as to prevent any recognition of their own children.

But most to be pitied were the poor waifs who were cast out to be the victims of the weather or of wild beast, or to be reared for slavery, and often the brothel, by any who might choose to bring them up to years of maturity. Aristotle advocated the inhuman custom of exposure. "Let it be the law," he said, "that nothing imperfect or maimed shall be brought up." Plutarch mentions "a sort of chasm" into which helpless infants were cast.

When the great Roman general Germanicus died, the event was commemorated by imposing civic and religious rites, and among the honors to the renowned dead were, says Suetonius the Latin historian, "new-born infants exposed." How different from the part taken by children in connection with the death of General Grant, upon whose coffin was affectionately laid by them a wreath of oak-leaves which they had gathered out of the woods, and which by direction of the family was proudly carried in the great funeral procession in New York, in one of the grandest pageants the world has ever witnessed!

What a transformation Christianity has wrought in the estimation placed upon childhood! Ever since the Babe of Bethlehem was cradled in a manger, and ever since as a man he said, "of such is the kingdom," little children have been more honored and more tenderly loved and nurtured. The parental relation has been dearer; motherhood has meant a great deal more. Unlike Plato's republic, which was inimical to childhood, unlike the pagan world generally with its exposure of infants, the millennium of Scripture is when "a little child shall lead them," while of the New Jerusalem the prophet says, "And the streets of the city shall be full of boys and girls playing in the streets thereof." Such instructions, coming with the authority of inspiration, have revolutionized public sentiment relative to infancy and childhood.

2. The Bible has also elevated woman. Grecian and Roman womanhood is not to be admired. To be sure, there were some pure and beautiful characters. Greece boasted a Penelope, who accepted the proposal of marriage from Ulysses by covering her face with a veil to hide her blushes, and who rejected all suitors during the twenty years' absence of her husband at the Trojan War, remaining faithful in the hope of his return, in which she was not disappointed. Rome, too, had a Cornelia, who in an early widowhood refused many advantageous offers (one from a king) that she might devote herself entirely to her children; and when a caller desired to see her jewelry, in her two boys, invited in for the purpose, she showed "her jewels." But

these are solitary examples. The prevailing type of womanhood was that of worldliness and wickedness, with no high aim in life. Dress and dinner-party, theatre and circus, absorbed the feminine attention.

A wife of Caligula the emperor on one wedding occasion wore a set of emeralds worth two millions of dollars. One of the wives of Nero, says Pliny, "was accustomed to have her daintier mules shod with gold." In the train of such unnatural extravagance followed immoralities and infidelities which finally broke up the family and destroyed the state.

The biblical idea of wedlock, the divine order of things, is indicated by the one man and one woman placed in Eden. God evidently intended marriage to be monogamous. Polygamy sprang up, and was practiced even by Old-Testament saints, but this was a departure from the original intent, and was expressly attributed to the hardness of the people's hearts by Christ, who restored the marriage relation to its primeval condition, making again the twain one.

Turn now to Greece, and what was its ideal relation between man and woman? Let Plato, the greatest of its moral philosophers, answer. In the portrayal of his model republic, in the description of his Utopia, he proposes a community of wives. "As among other animals, so also among men," is the exact wording of the plan. We stand aghast at the proposition, and especially when he writes calmly of improving the race after the manner of the methods pursued with "hunting-dogs" and "birds." With such teaching from the highest sources it is not strange that the prominent women of Greece, the companions of statesmen and philosophers, were the Aspasias and Phrynes, persons who would not be tolerated in decent society at present. Such at that time had their witty sayings collected, and statues were erected to their memory by an admiring public. The wife, on the contrary, sank into obscurity. She was relegated to practical slavery. She was made to feel her inferiority. "Is there a human being," asks Socrates, "with whom you talk less than with your wife?" And he used to go and talk with one of the women of the town. Perhaps Xantippe was not altogether to blame for her exhibitions of temper.

In Rome it was no better. There had once been domestic excellence. Indeed, the claim was that there were no divorces for the first five hundred years of Roman history. But in the first century of our era such a state of innocence was only a dim and distant memory, and hence Juvenal says:

"Yes, I believe that chastity was known
And prized on earth while Saturn filled the throne,
When rocks a bleak and scanty shelter gave,
When sheep and shepherds thronged one common cave,
And when the mountain-wife her couch bestrewed
With skins of beasts, joint tenants of the wood,
And reeds, and leaves plucked from the neighboring tree."

He had reason for such a lamentation, since, according to his testimony, the nuptial garlands were not faded often till marriage had given place to divorce, and since one woman could have had this truthful inscription on her tomb, "*eight husbands in five years.*" Cicero divorced his wife with whom he had lived thirty years, and married a young woman of wealth, whom in turn he discarded. Martial, who was born a few years after the Saviour's death, mentions in one of his epigrams a woman who married her tenth husband within a month. Seneca, contemporary with Paul, makes the astounding declaration that there are "distinguished women of noble families" who "reckon their years not by the number of the consuls, but by that of their husbands." Of course the wife sank under such circumstances. She became unworthy of notice. Not so very incredible, therefore, is the information given by Plutarch of a member of the Senate expelled from that body "because," such is the historian's precise language, "in the presence of his daughter and in open day he had kissed his wife." The lordly Roman, no more than the Grecian, would not have approved of the sentiment of Scripture:

"Her husband also, and he praiseth her, saying,
Many daughters have done virtuously,
But thou excellest them all."

According to the pagan idea, the wife was to receive

no appreciative word or caress. She was to be kept suitably humble. By cold neglect she was to be taught her lower position in the scale of being. Then in the name of a hospitable friendship between families, and under the form of religious worship within the very temples, prevailed the most abominable practices, of which it would be a shame even to speak. The conjugal relation was thus destroyed, divorces became easy and immorality swept away the family.

Christianity wrought a great transformation. It elevated women to companionship. Our Lord did not disdain their ministrations. He honored them by appearing to them first after the resurrection. Paul rejoiced to find in them his first converts, and taught that there was in Christianity neither male nor female. They felt a new dignity in being thus recognized, and they rose under the encouragement step by step, until Libanius, the cultured friend of the apostate emperor Julian, once exclaimed, "What women there are among the Christians!" Such was the judgment of even a pagan as to the elevating influence of Bible-teaching upon womanhood.

3. Consider next how nations have been lifted by the religion of the Bible from barbarism. Wherever the Scriptures are read, and only there, do we see a high order of civilization. Take European countries, and we find enlightenment graded according to the knowledge that each has of God's

word. Heathen nations begin to wake up intellectually and commercially as soon as they are given the Scriptures. The Sandwich Islands and Madagascar are striking examples of the elevating influence of the Bible. Nor will it do to attribute the changed condition of things to the general spirit of progress. Let a mining-town in the very midst of civilization be for a succession of years without the preached word, and how soon the people degenerate, until there is a reign of terror, of gambling, of drunkenness, of lust, of anarchy! But let the gospel be introduced, and communities begin improving; and it is the same with nations.

Let us trace the development under biblical teaching of a single great nation, the English. When Cæsar landed in Britain, 55 B. C., he found the inhabitants to be savages, with "clothing of skins." Sometimes they were not as richly attired as that even, for, in the language of Cowper,

"Time was when clothing sumptuous or for use,
Save their own painted skins, our sires had none."

When the Roman general Suetonius about 60 A. D. proposed to conquer Britain, he was surprised at the wild appearance of the natives lining the shore and ready to fight. Women mingled with the soldiers, and, swinging their flaming torches and tossing their disheveled hair, they ran backward and forward and shrieked like incarnate fiends. The Britons were nothing less than savage tribes. Their religion was the veriest superstition. Sometimes their priests, the Druids, offered up human victims to the imaginary deities. How could people be reclaimed from such degradation? Why, the religion of the Bible was introduced, and, says Hume himself, they made great "advances toward arts and civil manners."

But just as they began to emerge from their barbarism there came apparent disaster in the immigration of a new and less-civilized element into the country. In the fifth century hordes of barbarians from the German forests crossed the sea and established themselves in Britain. These Angles and Saxons divided the country up among themselves into seven separate kingdoms. Who were these Anglo-Saxons, from whom, as well as from the Britons, we are descended? They were heathen tribes which fought each other, much as our Indians have done. Fighting was their main occupation for several generations, but their contests were of so little account as hardly to deserve historical mention. Indeed, Milton, according to Hume, says "that the skirmishes of kites and crows as much merited a particular narrative as the confused transactions and battles of the Saxon Heptarchy;" and the historian Knight speaks of their fierce hostilities and treacherous alliances affecting us "little more than the wars and truces of Choctaws and Cherokees."

Such were the Anglo-Saxons, who were below

the Britons even in point of civilization. They nearly extirpated the Christian religion, thereby causing the country to revert, says Hume, to its "ancient barbarity." Macaulay refers to their coarseness in his allusion to their "huge piles of food and hogsheads of strong drink." They had but little more refinement than brutes. All that was fair about them was their physical features. They had long flaxen hair and blooming countenances, but mentally, socially and morally they were very inferior, and the cultivated Roman looked upon them about as we look upon the negroes of Central Africa. Indeed, these heathen ancestors of ours were bought and sold as slaves, as the Africans have been in later times.

Connected with this fact is the familiar but ever-romantic story of what led to their evangelization and civilization. A pious abbot was strolling along the streets of Rome. He stopped at the market-place to witness the sales. Some slaves were on the auction-block, and he was struck by their fresh, beautiful faces, and when, upon inquiring their nationality, he was told that they were Angles, he replied with that famous pun which has come down the centuries, that they would more properly be denominated angels; and he was interested at once in their religious welfare. When he afterward sat on the pontifical throne as Gregory the Great he resolved to send missionaries to them in their distant island home.

ELEVATING INFLUENCE OF THE BIBLE. 147

That is the kind of ancestors we had, and if it had not been for the cause of Christian or foreign missions we would be sitting in pagan darkness, for their religion was gross beyond conception. They had numerous gods, to whom they sacrificed not only animals, but human beings. Their chief deity was the god of war, and hence the better fighters they were the more religious they were. Their idea of Paradise was that of a vast hall where they could recline on couches and drink ale from the skulls of their slain enemies.

But the religion of the Bible was carried to these debased Anglo-Saxons. One of their chiefs, King Ethelbert of Kent, had married a French princess who was a Christian, and Queen Bertha was allowed the free exercise of her religion. This was the opportune time chosen by Gregory, but when his forty missionaries, headed by Augustine, got as far as France, they heard such frightful things about those to whom they were going, fearful as the stories of modern cannibalism, that they begged to be released from the perilous mission. They, however, were urged to proceed with their lives in their hands, and they did brave the peril. When they reached Britain (597 A. D.) they sought an audience with King Ethelbert of Kent. The cautious monarch received them in the open air, lest they should influence him by some sort of magic. He kept them at a safe distance. He guarded against being mesmerized or bewitched by the strange foreigners, who, however, gradually disarmed him of fear and gained his confidence, till eventually he became a convert to Christianity, his wife's religion. Thus was the gospel introduced again among our pagan ancestors, and even the great infidel historian of England pronounces this event "the most memorable" in the reign of that king. The leaven spread to the other divisions of the Heptarchy, and in 664 A. D. a union was brought about between the various branches of the Anglo-Saxon Church; and this prepared the way for that political union in 827 A. D., when, under Egbert, the seven independent kingdoms were consolidated and the united country was first called Angle-land—that is, England—and the English race started on its march of amazing progress.

What lifted those warring tribes out of heathenism and developed and cemented them into a great people? The Bible. Into Britons and Anglo-Saxons life from above was breathed, and the mightiest, grandest people of all history sprung into being. Every new incursion of Danes or Normans was taken up under the power of the gospel and utilized as fresh blood to be sent coursing through the body politic. There have been revolutions now and then, but these have been only the eruptions which have left the nation healthier and stronger. Territory has been added to territory, till English-speaking people to-day control a scope of country simply colossal in extent, the sun never setting on the worldwide dominion and England's drum-beat being literally heard around the globe. Art, science, civilization and Christianity keep pace with the onward movement of this great political power. Isaiah grows eloquent over the little one becoming a thousand, and the small one a strong nation, through the Lord's hastening, and he breaks out, "Who are these that fly as a cloud, and as the doves to their windows? Surely the isles shall wait for Me, and the ships of Tarshish first." The prophet seems almost to have seen the white-sailed fleets of the British isles riding proudly every sea, speeding over vast expanses of water with the rapid flight of white doves before a storm, and with the velocity of the cloud borne swiftly along by cyclonic wind. Out of savage Britons and heathen Anglo-Saxons, out of piratical Danes and semi-civilized Normans, has been wrought by the religion of the Bible that which we do see. God's word has been the lamp and light by which this national progress has been made. To whatever nation it goes it has the same elevating influence, and even Darwin, after seeing the transformation wrought by the gospel on certain isles of the sea, became a regular contributor to the cause, and testified, "The lesson of the missionary is that of the enchanter's wand." Let, then, this magical book be sent around the globe. Glad are we that it has been rendered into three hundred and sixty tongues and dialects by the British and American Bible societies, and let there be no halt in the good work till the "blest volume" has been carried in the vernacular to every kindred, every tribe, on this terrestrial ball. Each of us may well say with Sir Walter Scott in his Journal, published in 1890, "I would, if called upon, die a martyr for the Christian religion, so completely is (in my poor opinion) its divine origin proved by its beneficial effects on the state of society."

CHAPTER XI.

THE BIBLE AND THE GOLDEN CITY OF BABYLON.

"The golden city ceased."—ISA. 14:4.

THE reference is to Babylon, and let us see how the word of God regarding it has been fulfilled. There is no more fascinating subject than the agreements of history and prophecy. The faith must be strengthened when prophets foretold events whose actual occurrence historians relate hundreds of years afterward. Babylon is only one of many illustrations of the exact correspondence between scriptural prediction and historical fact.

The former glory of the city and its present desolation can hardly be overstated. It is well described by Isaiah as the "golden city" and as "the lady of kingdoms" and as the "beauty of the Chaldeans' pride." Herodotus, two hundred and fifty years later and an eye-witness, says: "Its extent, its beauty and its magnificence surpass all that has come within my knowledge." According to this writer, it was laid out in a square each of whose sides was fifteen miles in length. That makes a grand total of two hundred and twenty-five square miles, whereas London has only one hundred and twenty-two square miles, and New York only forty-one. Chicago itself, with its one hundred and seventy-four square miles since the recent annexations which make it the largest city in *area* in the world, is not so large as ancient Babylon was.

The glory of the city was augmented in that, according to a Roman historian (Quintus Rufus Curtius), nine-tenths of all the enclosed space consisted of gardens and meadows and parks. It was even said to contain tillable land enough to support its inhabitants in a time of siege. It was a great country-city. Its streets crossed each other at right angles, and were one hundred and fifty feet broad, and were lined with elegant residences three and four stories high.

Its political supremacy was once such that Jeremiah could call it the "hammer of the whole earth," to "break in pieces" whatever it smote. When the Mohammedans in the eighth century swept over Spain, and were moving on to the conquest of Europe, there met the hitherto invincible Moslems a hero who dealt such sturdy blows that he has ever since been known as Charles Martel, which, being interpreted, is "Charles the Hammer." The vigor of his arm beat back the Saracen power and saved Christendom. He struck hard and gained a proud title, which, however, Babylon centuries before had won in that it was called the "hammer of the whole earth."

But what was to be the fate of this strong and beautiful city? Hear the language of Jeremiah: "And Babylon shall become heaps, a dwelling-place for jackals, an astonishment, and an hissing, without inhabitant." No less explicit was Isaiah, who said, "It shall never be inhabited, neither shall it be dwelt in from generation to generation: neither shall the Arabian pitch tent there; neither shall shepherds make their flocks to lie down there. But wild beasts of the desert shall lie there; and their houses shall be full of doleful creatures; and ostriches shall dwell there, and satyrs shall dance there. And wolves shall cry in their castles, and jackals in the pleasant palaces." Has this utter forsakenness overtaken the golden city? As early as 20 B. C., Strabo speaks of the site of Babylon as a "vast desolation." Jerome in the fourth century of our era declares that it was the hunting-ground of the Persian monarchs. Rawlinson in his *Ancient Monarchies* says: "Vast heaps or mounds, shapeless and unsightly, are scattered at intervals over the entire region where it is certain that Babylon anciently stood." Do you wish the testimony of an eminent archæologist who has personally been on the ground and explored the ruins? "The site of Babylon," says Layard, "is a naked and hideous waste." "Owls," he says, "start from the scanty thickets, and the foul jackal stalks through the furrows." An English consul (C. J. Rich, 1811) testifies: "There are many dens of wild beasts in various parts, in one of which I found the bones of sheep and other animals, and perceived a strong smell like that of a lion. I also found quantities of porcupine-quills, and in most of the cavities are numbers of bats and owls." Verily the golden city has ceased!

If we enter into details, we shall see the same wonderful verification of the word spoken of old by the Lord. There is not merely a general, but there is a specific, fulfillment of the prophetic.

1. One of the marked features of Babylon was its system of irrigation. Through the centre of the city flowed the Euphrates, a river a quarter of a mile wide, "and its depth such," said Xenophon, "that of two men standing, the one upon the other, the uppermost would not appear above the water. So that the river afforded a better defense to the city than its walls." Canals, broad and sometimes navigable, were cut in every direction. An immense artificial lake was dug west of the city. This was thirty-five feet deep and one hundred and sixty miles in circuit, or forty miles square. Into this the whole river could be turned if at any time a dry river-bed was desired for mechanical constructions. Very properly was the city thus addressed by Jeremiah: "O thou that dwellest upon many waters," while the Jewish captives said plaintively,

> "By the rivers of Babylon,
> There we sat down, yea, we wept,
> When we remembered Zion."

But what said Jehovah of this extensive system of irrigation?—"I will dry up her sea, and make her fountain dry." Long ago Diodorus, of the age of the first Cæsars, referred to the canals being filled with alluvial deposits, while what had been a fertile garden was converted into a marsh; and it remains to this day, according to the modern traveler, a "desert," no longer blossoming as the rose.

2. Take, again, those walls which Herodotus says were over three hundred feet high and over eighty feet wide—those walls upon which, between the battlements, four-horse chariots could meet and pass without colliding. Consider also those hundred gates of brass which the father of historians mentions. Surely such substantial works would endure. Nay, Jeremiah cries, "her walls are thrown down." This prophet is still more definite when he says, "The broad walls of Babylon shall be utterly overthrown, and her high gates shall be burned with fire." Have those splendid fortifications survived in spite of Heaven's malediction? Listen to a recent visitor (Bishop J. P. Newman) to these historic scenes: "To-day can be seen, and only here and there, low, shapeless, detached mounds where once the proud walls stood." Our very Bible Dictionary says: "Babylon has been a quarry from which all the tribes in the vicinity have

perpetually derived the bricks with which they have built their cities." The fortifications are all gone.

3. But there was a massive temple in the city. Has it, like the Pantheon of Rome, come down to the present?

It is Herodotus who tells us of a temple of the god Bel eight stories high, with a winding staircase running around the outside clear to the top, which was surmounted by statues, one of them forty feet in height. Here treasures are said to have accumulated to the estimated value of more than six hundred millions of dollars. Here, we learn from the sacred historian, were stored the vessels taken from Jerusalem, for the record reads, " Nebuchadnezzar also carried off the vessels of the house of the Lord to Babylon, and put them in his temple at Babylon." This may have been the tower of Babel, which, you recollect, was to "reach unto heaven," and, though it was not completed at the time on account of the confusion of tongues, it appears to have been a cherished project afterward, for Isaiah seems to have it in mind when he represents Babylon as saying, "I will ascend into heaven, I will exalt my throne above the stars of God."[9] This temple of Bel is described by Herodotus, who makes it rise to the height of six hundred feet, which is higher than St. Peter's at Rome (four hundred and forty-eight feet), or St. Paul's at London (four hundred and four feet), or the Cathedral at Strasburg (four hundred and sixty-one feet), or the Capitol at Washington (three hundred and fifty feet), or the Washington Monument (five hundred and fifty-five feet); it is surpassed in height only by the Eiffel Tower at Paris, which springs into the air one thousand feet.

What says prophecy of this imposing structure of old devoted to the degrading and licentious worship of the god Bel? Jeremiah exclaims, "Babylon is taken, Bel is put to shame"; "And I will do judgment upon Bel in Babylon, and I will bring forth out of his mouth that which he hath swallowed up." Did this receiver of rich treasures have to disgorge? Herodotus says that Xerxes plundered this temple. Ezra says, "And the gold and silver vessels also of the house of God, which Nebuchadnezzar took out of the temple that was at Jerusalem, and brought them into the temple of Babylon, those did Cyrus the king take *out* of the temple of Babylon." Some at least of the six hundred millions of treasures which had been swallowed up were taken by Xerxes, and the holy vessels which had been swallowed up were removed at the command of Cyrus and restored to Jerusalem. Well did Isaiah prophesy, "Bel boweth down," while Jeremiah declared, "Though Babylon should mount up to heaven, and though she should fortify the height of her strength, yet from me shall spoilers come unto her, saith the Lord;" and it was even so. Not even the completed tower of Babel, not even this temple of Bel with its eight stories towering up to an altitude of nearly six hundred feet, not even this splendid edifice of the golden city, could resist the decree of God, for the traveler of to-day (Bishop Newman) sees it in the mound, Birs Nimroud, " rising suddenly out of the desert plain, a riven, fragmentary, blasted pile," looming " up a vast mass of shapeless ruins, as when, by some mighty convulsion of nature, temples are thrown on temples and towers are piled on towers." Such are the words of one who has been an observer of what he so vividly portrays. Verily Bel exalted to heaven has bowed down. So utter was the ruin that when Alexander the Great visited it he employed ten thousand men two months to clear away the rubbish preparatory to rebuilding, and then the task was abandoned while yet a beginning had scarcely been made.[10]

4. The palace of Nebuchadnezzar (the modern Kasr) has fared no better—the palace whose outer circumference was six miles, whose inner walls were of colored bricks upon which were depicted such hunting-scenes as a man thrusting his spear through a lion and a woman on horseback hurling her lance at a leopard—fitting representations for a city founded by Nimrod the mighty hunter.

Within this palace were the famous "hanging gardens," covering three and a half acres, erected by the king for his homesick queen, who had come from a mountainous country and who longed for the hills of her native land. She had an artificial hill made for her with a succession of terraces, each watered by machinery drawing the supply up from the Euphrates, and distributing it to delicate flowers and to enormous trees rooted in hollow piers filled with mould. By marble steps the queen could ascend this mountain, which towered above the high walls in the most picturesque manner; she could recline during the heat of the day in romantic arbors on the hillside. Like Nero's celebrated Golden House, which contained within its spacious area cornfields, woods and a lake, Nebuchadnezzar's palace contained a mountain.

It may have been here where Nebuchadnezzar walked and viewed the city when he said, " Is not this great Babylon which I have built for the royal dwelling-place by the might of my power and for the glory of my majesty?" It was for his impiety on this occasion that he was stricken with insanity, to wander for a while a lunatic, perhaps on this very mountain, his body wet with the dew of heaven, his hair grown like eagles' feathers, his nails like birds' claws, while he ate grass as oxen. It was probably in this palace with its hanging gardens that Belshazzar feasted a thousand of his lords, and saw on the wall, not a hunting-scene, but the fingers of a man's hand writing his death-sentence. It may have been here where Daniel faced both these great monarchs, and told them boldly of their sins; and to commemorate possibly his rescue from the den of lions he may have seen in some conspicuous spot the still-existing sculptured lion, about thirteen feet long and ten feet high, standing over a prostrate man with outstretched arms; he may have seen this great work of art which has been unearthed in these latter days. Grander than the temple of Bel was this palace with its artificial mountain, which the Greeks called one of the seven wonders of the world.

And did prophecy doom this to destruction? It is Jeremiah who speaks thus in the name of the Lord: "Behold, I am against thee, O destroying *mountain*, saith the Lord, which destroyest all the earth: and I will stretch out mine hand upon thee, and roll thee down from the rocks, and I will make thee a burnt mountain." Such was the prediction. What is the fact according to present explorations? The one from whom we have quoted before, and who has stood on the very site of the once superb palace, says: "Everywhere were shapeless mounds, covered with fragments of glass, marble, pottery, and inscribed bricks, mingled with a white nitrous soil whose blanched appearance completed the picture of desolation."

5. Once more, the very method of the city's capture, which led to its final destruction, is foretold. Isaiah says, "Desolation shall come upon thee suddenly, which thou knowest not"; "Thus saith the Lord to his anointed, to Cyrus, . . . The gates shall not be shut. . . . And I will give thee

the treasures of darkness." Jeremiah says, "I have laid a snare for thee, and thou art also taken, O Babylon, and thou wast not aware"; "Surely I will fill thee with men, as with the canker-worm; and they shall lift up a shout against thee"; "One post shall run to meet another, and one messenger to meet another, to show the king of Babylon that his city is taken in every quarter: and the passages are surprised;" "And I will make drunk her princes and wise men, her governors and her deputies, and her mighty men; and they shall sleep a perpetual sleep, and not wake." Such are the predictions uttered more than a hundred years before Babylon fell.

What are the facts? Whether Cyrus himself was the divine instrument, or—which is more probable—whether, as Professor Ladd claims, "the name of Cyrus in Isaiah is used as a title of the Persian monarchs in general," and whether thus, as is likely, Darius was the one who took the city by the well-known stratagem,—Rawlinson the historian gives the substantial facts as follows: "When all was prepared Cyrus determined to wait for the arrival of a certain festival, during which the whole populace were wont to engage in drinking and reveling, and then silently in the dead of night to turn the water of the river and make his attack. . . . Drunken riot and mad excitement held possession of the town: the siege was forgotten; ordinary precautions were neglected. . . . In silence and darkness the Persians watched at the two points where the Euphrates entered and left the walls. Anxiously they noted the gradual sinking of the water. . . . At last shadowy forms began to emerge from the obscurity of the deep river-bed, and on the landing-places opposite the river-gates scattered clusters of men grew into solid columns; the undefended gateways were seized; a war-shout was raised; the alarm was taken and spread. . . . In the darkness and confusion of the night a terrible massacre ensued. The drunken revelers could make no resistance. . . . Bursting into the palace, a band of Persians made their way to the presence of the monarch and slew him on the scene of his impious revelry. Other bands carried fire and sword through the town. When morning came Cyrus found himself undisputed master of the city." Thus and there were all the minutiæ of prophetic utterance fulfilled; thus and there died Belshazzar. There two centuries later died Alexander the Great in a similar revel, after trying in vain to rebuild the city, its canals, walls, temple and palace. He knew not that the decree had gone forth—"the golden city ceased."

Babylon the great has for ever fallen. Prophecy has become history, and the word of God standeth sure, and, blessed be his name, "the Lord knoweth them that are his." We can have unfailing confidence in our God, who will bring to pass whatever he has promised as well as threatened. No golden city even, no principalities or powers of the wicked one, can thwart his great purpose with reference to his redeemed children. He shall bring them out of the great tribulation. He shall gather his elect out of a world that is passing away. What encouragement here for Christians! and what warning to the unconverted, who are certain to be overwhelmed at last! The golden city could not withstand God, who swept it " with the besom of destruction." So shall it be with the unrighteous, but God's people are eternally safe. They are journeying to a golden city which shall never cease—a city of jasper walls, with foundations of all manner of precious stones, with gates of pearl, whose builder and maker is God.

CHAPTER XII.

THE BIBLE AND THE COMMERCIAL CITY OF TYRE.

"Who is there like Tyre, like her that is brought to silence in the midst of the sea?"—Ezek. 27:32.

WE are to consider this commercial city at certain great epochs, and we are to see how various prophecies have been fulfilled in her history. Ezekiel devotes nearly three chapters, Isaiah one chapter and other prophets a few verses to portraying the future of Tyre. They all predict the utter desolation that was to come, and our text might have constituted the sad refrain of each of the inspired writers: "Who is there like Tyre, like her that is brought to silence in the midst of the sea?"

I. Such a fate seemed unlikely in view of the prosperity and splendor of the city at the time of the deliverance of the prophecies.

1. Tyre was situated on the eastern coast of the Mediterranean, being built both on the mainland and on an adjoining island half a mile distant, and it was in the latter position that her strength and

glory specially consisted. She might have been called, as Venice has been, "the bride of the sea." She is addressed as "at the entry of the sea" and as "in the heart of the seas," and as "the stronghold of the sea." She could not, however, conceive of such a misfortune as being "brought to silence in the midst of the sea."

She had stood for centuries, and she seemed absolutely secure for all time. She boasted of her antiquity, as is evident from the question which Isaiah said would be asked in subsequent ages: "Is this your joyous city, whose antiquity is of ancient days?" She could point to a hoary and venerable past. She could have told the author of our text that a thousand years before Joshua had spoken of "the fenced city of Tyre." She could have reminded the prophet that four hundred years back her sovereign, Hiram, was called upon by Solomon for help in building the temple. When Herodotus visited her, a hundred years later than Ezekiel's time, this father of historians, who went to see the famous temple erected to Hercules in that city, was told by the Tyrian priests "that from the building of Tyre two thousand and three hundred years had elapsed." With so many centuries of happy existence the proud city would naturally be incredulous as to her predicted downfall. She was accustomed to say, "I am a god, I sit in the seat of God, in the midst of the seas."

Being sea-girt, she considered herself as impregnable as mighty Sidon, whose daughter she was, and whose citizens the sacred writer had in mind when he spoke of people dwelling "in security, after the manner of the Zidonians, quiet and secure; for there was none in the land, possessing authority, that might put them to shame in anything." That is the way the Tyrians felt—absolutely secure because of their insular position.

2. Besides, they were strongly fortified. We know what their walls must have been from a single stone which has remained to this day, and which measures seventeen feet in length and six and a half feet in thickness. Furthermore, in recent explorations at Jerusalem a shaft has been sunk eighty feet, and the foundations laid by Solomon have been disclosed, and some of these stones are twenty to twenty-six feet long. With reference to these we are informed (Wright's *Ancient Cities*): "The calcium light revealed upon them Phœnician numerals, letters and other signs in red paint, which are supposed to be quarry-marks made by Hiram's masons." If the Tyrians were skillful enough to transport all the way to Jerusalem such immense stones, we may be sure their fortifications were massive, and sufficiently so to make their overthrow apparently impossible.

3. Thus secure from surrounding water and mortar, Tyre prosecuted business with an enterprise and success that have never been surpassed. Ezekiel gives a whole chapter to describing her

commerce, and he seems to weave in all the geographical names then known to show the extent of her traffic with the nations of earth. Well did Isaiah call her merchants "princes," for they bought and sold everywhere. They sailed the Black Sea, and returned, if not with golden fleeces for which the first Argonauts sought, at least with rich treasures. They had long before manned Solomon's ships, which sped down the Red Sea, and brought back from India not only the gold of Ophir, but also all manner of curious things, such as apes and peacocks, which had never been seen before in Palestine, and which created a great sensation there. The Tyrians had to furnish the sailors for these celebrated expeditions, and they never ceased to enrich themselves from the distant lands.

They had gone all over the Mediterranean. They had planted a powerful colony at Carthage in Northern Africa. They had extracted wealth from the mines of Spain, till their ships of Tarshish became as well known as England's East Indiamen are to-day. They are said to have found silver in such abundance that they did not have room to store it away in their vessels, and that they might utilize every inch of space they are said to have used the precious metal for their anchors. At any rate, according to Ezekiel, the rowing "benches" were of "ivory," while "fine linen with broidered work from Egypt" constituted their "sails," and the ship's "awning" was made of "blue and purple from the isles."

Nay, their gay merchantmen ventured out through the Pillars of Hercules; they ran the very gauntlet of what was then a Gibraltar indeed as they moved out into the great and almost unknown Atlantic. Diodorus Siculus tells of their reaching what seemed to them the Isles of the Blest, and the Azores or Canaries in their tropical beauty must have seemed the "dwelling of gods rather than of men." They are believed to have gone clear to the British isles, and to have gotten tin at Cornwall, and Herodotus speaks of their getting tin from "the ends of the earth," although he was incredulous about what were called the Tin Islands (Cassiterides).

Nor could he credit what was a fact, that these adventurous navigators before his day had sailed down the Red Sea, and that they had actually gone round the southernmost point of Africa, and had made their way back through the straits opening from the Atlantic into the Mediterranean. He related how on his visit to Tyre the Tyrians had told him of their having reached a point where the sun was always north of them, where the shadows were always cast in one direction. "For my part," he says, "I do not believe them"; and yet what they told him about the sun was positive proof that they had rounded the cape, thus anticipating by more than two thousand years Vasco da Gama, who by the same exploit in these comparatively modern times so astonished all Europe and gained undying fame. The Tyrians were ahead of him by only two millenniums; that is all. So long ago did they thoroughly understand the seas which they rode in triumph everywhere, while they made their city the wealthiest that ever existed as they gathered from far and near silver and gold, iron, tin and lead, emeralds, rubies, diamonds and "all precious stones." All these the prophet mentions, besides " choice wares, in wrappings of blue and broidered work, and in chests of rich apparel bound with cords."

There ought to be mentioned also the city's great industry of extracting dye from shellfish, her factories for this purpose being so numerous, according to Strabo, as to fill the air with an unpleasant odor. But a vast revenue was derived from this source. Any article bearing the delicate coloring of Tyrian skill was in universal demand. Juvenal speaks of "Tyrian tapestry" as something particularly fine. Virgil speaks of the luxury of "Tyrian purple" for sleeping apartments. Homer, ages before, had sung of

"Belts
That, rich with Tyrian dye, refulgent glowed."

While Tyre became the richest and most splendid city of antiquity, "the mart of nations," she pursued her commercial ends with such selfishness and with such utter disregard of God that she was doomed to destruction. She had a form of godliness. She built a magnificent temple on her island, and this wonder of the world was what specially drew Herodotus to the city, and he was full of admiration for two colossal columns of gold and emerald which adorned the beautiful structure. He may have been mistaken in the material, but the appearance was that of two massive pillars of gold and emerald. So that the Tyrians had a form of godliness; they had a house of worship which must have rivaled Solomon's temple—which must have equaled, if it did not surpass, the finest edifices in which the wealthy now meet.

But they worshiped Mammon more than the true God, those Tyrians did, as people often do yet. They left no stone unturned to heap up riches. So selfishly did they seek gain that it is said (*American Cyclopædia*) if a Phœnician merchantman bound for some land of mineral wealth should find that a Roman ship was following, the master of the Tyrian vessel would run his craft upon the rocks, so as to lead the other to destruction, and on returning home the loyal citizens of Tyre would have his loss made good by the city; so determined was she that other people should not learn of her sources of wealth. The story is not incredible when we are informed by the prophet that at the destruction of Jerusalem on a certain occasion Tyre said exultingly, "Aha, she is broken that was the gate of the peoples; she is turned unto me: I shall be replenished, now that she is laid waste." It was for this unworthy spirit that the doom of Tyre was pronounced. She was to be utterly destroyed, until the lamentation should be, " Who is there like Tyre, like her that is brought to silence in the midst of the sea ?"

II. We will now turn to see how the city, notwithstanding her strong insular position and her antiquity, notwithstanding her massive walls, notwithstanding all her resources which she possessed as "the stronghold of the sea," how in spite of everything and contrary to all human probability, was finally leveled to the ground. We will note the successive steps by which her ruin was accomplished. There was wheel within wheel, but the divine purpose went straight forward.

1. The prophecies were fulfilled in part by the siege of Nebuchadnezzar. The protracted nature of this siege was foretold when Ezekiel said, "Every head was made bald, and every shoulder was peeled." Was this the fact? Josephus, on the authority of both Greek and Phœnician histories, states that the siege continued thirteen years. Even then it is said, by way of prediction, "yet had he no wages." Was the siege practically without result? was it without the usual spoil for the conqueror? It is not certain that the city was really taken. Or if it was, it may have been so impoverished as to have proved disappointing to the greed of the victor, who naturally would have had great expectations with reference to a city reputed to be very opulent.

But Jerome would seem to give the best explanation of there being "no wages." He says, on the authority of Assyrian histories, that when the Tyrians found further resistance would be useless, "they went on board their ships, and fled to Carthage or to some islands of the Ionian and Ægean seas"; and he adds that they took their valuables along. They were not, therefore, totally destroyed yet—not yet, in the words of the text, "brought to silence in the midst of the sea." But they were humbled under the mighty hand of Nebuchadnezzar. It was not intended in the providence of God that utter desolation should come at once.

Isaiah had expressed the extent of the humbling when he said, "Tyre shall be forgotten seventy years"; that is, she was to share with the Jews the Babylonian captivity. "And it shall come to pass after the end of seventy years," the prophet continues, "that the Lord will visit Tyre, and she shall return to her hire," even with "all the kingdoms of the world." This also corresponds with the actual course of events.

2. The city did renew her prosperity, and two centuries later she thought she was strong enough to defy Alexander the Great as she had done the Assyrian. She was not only seagirt, but she was surrounded with walls which were one hundred and fifty feet high on the side of the island next to the mainland. The brilliant defence which she made is a matter of familiar history. In resisting the great Macedonian in 332 B. C., even more than

in opposing the Assyrian in 585, did she show her heroism. The later siege was only seven months as against the several years previously, but the struggle was more terrific.

Alexander proceeded to construct a huge mole from the continent to the island, but no sooner did it appear above the water than it was furiously assaulted, and a fire-ship, driven into it, spread havoc, and a storm arose to assist in the demolition of the causeway, which sank out of sight in the raging sea. Again it was slowly built with great trees and rocks and earth, until it for ever closed the gap between continental and insular Tyre, and along it were pushed the engines of war, while a large fleet moved from the sea upon the fortifications; and, though even then the conqueror wavered in his resolution because of the strength of the city, he at length after a fearful conflict won the day.

And were there any specific prophecies fulfilled? It had been predicted, "They shall lay thy stones and thy timber and thy dust in the midst of the waters." In Quintus Curtius or in Rollin we can read that the portions of the city on the mainland were used to construct the mole or causeway to the island, and thus the stones and timber and dust of the city were literally laid "in the midst of the waters." From the same historians we learn that the city was fired, and thus the words of Amos came true: "I will send a fire on the wall of Tyre, and it shall devour the palaces thereof"; and Zechariah's prediction was verified: "The Lord will dispossess her, and he will smite her power in the sea; and she shall be devoured with fire."

Then Joel had prophesied: "The children also of Judah and the children of Jerusalem have ye sold unto the sons of the Grecians, that ye might remove them from their border: behold, I will stir them up out of the place whither ye have sold them, and will return your recompense upon your own head; and I will sell *your* sons and your daughters." This unequivocal prediction was uttered four hundred and fifty years before Alexander's capture of Tyre, and the exasperated general did sell thirty thousand into slavery from that single city. In this connection it is "interesting to read on a clay tablet found at Nineveh," says Dr. W. B. Wright, "the contract of a Tyrian merchant with an Assyrian lady for the sale of two Hebrew slaves." But for such iniquity the Tyrians were sold into slavery by the destroyer of their city. Joel (800 B. C.) denounced the Tyrians for selling the Hebrews, and yet a Ninevite tablet now in the British Museum informs us that July 20, 709 B. C., a century after the prophet's reproval, a Phœnician sold to a woman of Nineveh two Hebrews for one hundred and thirty-five dollars. But the predicted recompense upon their own heads came when thirty thousand in captured Tyre were sold into bondage by Alexander.

Nay, those who fled, as they had done before, to Carthage and other colonial possessions around the Mediterranean only fulfilled Isaiah's prophecy, which says: "Arise, pass over to Kittim; even there shalt thou have no rest." Of Tyre's chief colony, the Carthaginians, it was sadly true that they had "no rest." With the three Punic wars which they waged through so many years with Rome, with such generals as Hannibal and Scipio to lead the respective armies, with the cry, "Carthago delenda est" ("Carthage must be destroyed") repeatedly awakening applause in the Roman Senate, —with such familiar facts of history, verily those who were driven forth from the merchant city had "no rest," not even in the isles of the sea, not even in the colonial possessions fringing the Mediterranean. Says Diodorus Siculus: "They prevented a part of their children and wives from falling into the hands of the enemy by sending them away secretly to the Carthaginians," but they did not prevent disaster coming to them even there.

3. And yet judgment was tempered with mercy. A blessing was predicted. Isaiah relieved the darkness of the future with a temporary gleam of light. He looked forward to a time when "her merchandise and her hire shall be holiness to the Lord: it shall not be treasured nor laid up; for her merchandise shall be for them that dwell before the Lord." She was not to be "brought to silence in the midst of the sea" till she had received the

gospel, and in a measure had accepted the same. Did that day ever come?

Among the "great multitude" who came to hear Jesus and to be healed of their diseases were, according to Luke, people from "Tyre and Sidon." It was in the "borders of Tyre and Sidon" that the "little daughter" of the "Syro-phœnician" woman was relieved by the Lord of a demoniacal possession. Paul "landed at Tyre," where he found "disciples," with whom he remained a week, and by whom, " with wives and children," he was accompanied to the ship at his departure, while they prayed together "on the beach" and bade each other a tender "farewell."

Subsequently Tyre became the seat of a Christian bishopric. There, in 324 A. D., Eusebius dedicated a fine cathedral, which he said he could not fittingly describe, "the grandeur that surpasses description, and the dazzling aspect of works glittering in the face of the speaker, the heights rising to the heavens." This ecclesiastical historian, commenting upon Isaiah's prophecy, says, "It is fulfilled in our time. For since a church of God hath been founded in Tyre as well as in other nations, many of its goods gotten by merchandise are consecrated to the Lord, being offered to his Church." Still later Jerome says: "We may behold churches in Tyre built to Christ; we may see their riches, that they are not laid up nor treasured, but given to those who dwell before the Lord."

4. But Jerome was astonished at the non-fulfillment of part of the prophecies. In the beginning of the fifth century of the Christian era he said Tyre was "the most noble and the most beautiful city of Phœnicia," and he asks how this can be made to agree with Ezekiel's prophecy, "Thou shalt be built no more." He did not seem to realize that centuries are required for the establishment of God's entire word. It was to be left, in the providence of God, to these later generations to witness the complete verification of the prophecy, that Tyre should be "brought to silence in the midst of the sea."

We will not speak of the Saracen conquest of the city, nor of its subsequent recovery by the Crusaders, nor of its humiliation again under the Turk. Suffice it to say that since 1561 there has been the sure and final decline. Did Ezekiel say, "I will make thee a bare rock: thou shalt be a place for the spreading of nets"? In 1697, Maundrell saw it a desolation indeed, the miserable inhabitants subsisting, he says, "chiefly upon fishing."

Did the prophet say that the stones of the city should lie "in the midst of the waters"? Says the scholarly Robinson in 1838, from personal observation: "The sole tokens of her more ancient splendor—columns of red and gray granite, sometimes forty or fifty heaped together, or marble pillars—lie broken and strewed beneath the waves in the midst of the sea." "Granite columns," says another observer (Dr. Thomson in his *Land and the Book*), "are thickly spread over the bottom of the sea on every side." Likewise we learn from Tristram, in his *Land of Israel*, that "for half a mile from the shore the sea flows to the depth of a foot or two over flat rocks covered by one mass of prostrate columns."

Does Ezekiel further say, "Thou shalt be no more: though thou be sought for, yet shalt thou never be found"? Renan confirms this. He writes: "A traveler who was not informed of its existence might pass along the whole coast without being aware that he was close to an ancient city."

With such facts before us we can take up the dirge of the text, "Who is there like Tyre, like her that is brought to silence in the midst of the sea?" Verily the word of the Lord does stand sure. Centuries may be required for its verification, but in the end every hostile power will be humbled, while the Church of God shall be preserved and exalted.

CHAPTER XIII.

BIBLICAL SIGNS PRECEDING THE DESTRUCTION OF JERUSALEM.

"And as some spake of the temple, how it was adorned with goodly stones and offerings, he said, As for these things which ye behold, the days will come in which there shall not be left here one stone upon another, that shall not be thrown down. And they asked him, saying, Master, when therefore shall these things be? and what shall be the sign when these things are about to come to pass?"—LUKE 21:5-7.

THE destruction of Jerusalem and of the temple therein by Titus in the year 70 A. D. was predicted by Christ about forty years before the event. The disciples were amazed at the prophecy, and they could hardly believe that it would be fulfilled. They asked the Master what signs would precede the great catastrophe, and he told them plainly, as he sat with them on Mount Olivet with the Holy City in full view and shining resplendent in the soft glow of a setting sun. Let us glance at history and see if the signs predicted with much detail did take place. It might be said, by way of introduction, that the signs seem to point primarily to the end of Jerusalem, and secondarily to the end of the world. There were, as Farrar has said, "two horizons, one near and one far off," while he adds that as the signs "did usher in the destruction of Jerusalem, so shall (they) reappear on a larger scale before the end of all things is at hand." Confining ourselves for the present to the dramatic ending of the Jewish polity and dispensation, we will consider the signs that were to precede that first great day of the Lord which is symbolic of a yet more dreadful day to come.

1. "Before all these things"—was one of the signs—"they shall lay their hands on you and shall persecute you." This prophecy certainly was most terribly fulfilled before the year 70, when Titus destroyed the city and temple. James was beheaded by Agrippa, and Paul by Nero, before that date. The history of the apostolic Church was one succession of religious persecutions. This is evident from the narrative of the Acts of the Apostles, and it is corroborated by profane history, which cannot be considered prejudiced in favor of Christianity. When the great fire broke out in Rome, continuing, says Suetonius, "six days and seven nights," until nearly half the city was burned down, Nero remarked upon "the beautiful effects of the conflagration." Now, this emperor himself was believed to have ordered the city to be fired, and, says Tacitus, "to suppress the rumor he falsely charged with the guilt and punished with the most exquisite tortures the persons commonly called Christians, who were hated for their enormities. Christus, the

founder of that name, was put to death as a criminal by Pontius Pilate, procurator of Judæa, in the reign of Tiberius: but the pernicious superstition, repressed for a time, broke out again, not only through Judæa, where the mischief originated, but through the city of Rome itself, whither all things horrible and disgraceful flow from all quarters as to a common receptacle, and where they are encouraged. Accordingly, first those were seized who confessed they were Christians; next, on their information, a vast multitude were convicted, not so much on the charge of burning the city as of hating the human race. And in their deaths they were also made the subjects of sport, for they were covered with the hides of wild beasts and worried to death by dogs, or nailed to crosses, or set fire to, and when day declined burned to serve for nocturnal lights." Such is the language, not of a Christian, but of a pagan, and of one whose life covered the latter half of the first century and the beginning of the second. The sign of religious persecution did then occur, and this very persecution, described by the Latin historian, raged six years before the destruction of Jerusalem.

2. A second most improbable sign was, "This gospel of the kingdom shall be preached in the whole world for a testimony unto all the nations; and then shall the end come." Have we any evidence that this sign preceded the destruction of Jerusalem? The Roman empire was recognized

in those days as comprising "the whole world," for of the decree by Cæsar Augustus Luke says, "All the world should be enrolled"; that is, the entire empire. Even with this limitation it would seem impossible that a religion whose Founder was crucified—a religion which antagonized all other religions by pronouncing them false—a religion which did not flatter men, but called them guilty sinners—a religion which required self-denial and sacrifice of life even—a religion which, after all, did not propose to propagate itself by force,—it would seem impossible that such a religion should be so widely diffused in forty years; but Christ staked his reputation on the prediction that before the destruction of Jerusalem, before 70 A. D., his gospel should be published in all the known world; and there is reason for believing that the prophecy proved true. Tacitus, in the quotation already made from him, says that the pernicious superstition was only suppressed in one place to break out in another, "not only through Judæa, where the mischief originated, but through the city of Rome itself, whither all things horrible and disgraceful flow." Pliny the Younger, who died about 116 A. D., writes: "Nor has the contagion of this superstition seized cities only, but the lesser towns also and the open country." Clement, who was a contemporary of Paul, says of that apostle, "He was a preacher both to the East and the West; he taught the whole world righteousness"; and Paul died before the year 70, previous to which Christ had said the gospel should be published among all nations. When he foretold the sign he had but a handful of followers, but the sign did not fail.

3. There were also to be great civil commotions—"wars and rumors of wars." Christ's advent was at a time of universal peace, the temple of Janus was closed. Nevertheless, there was to be within a generation the wildest disorder in governmental affairs; so he prophesied, at least.

Turning now for the period in question to Tacitus, and running over the contents of his *Annals*, we see such expressions as these: "Disturbances in Germany," "commotions in Africa," "commotions in Thrace," "insurrections in Gaul," "intrigues among the Parthians," "the war in Britain," "war in Armenia." So too from Josephus we learn what upheavals there were throughout the empire. "In all Syria," he says, the disorders were terrible; "every city was divided into two armies," Syrians and Jews; "so the daytime was spent in shedding of blood, and the night in fear." We are told that it was "common to see cities filled with dead bodies still lying unburied, and those of old men mixed with infants; . . . women also lay among them." No wonder with the dead thus scattered about promiscuously Josephus could only call the calamities inexpressible. Thirteen thousand were slain in Scythopolis. Ten thousand at Damascus had their "throats cut." Twenty thousand were killed "in one hour's time" at Cæsarea. In Alexandria neither old nor young were spared till fifty thousand lay dead in "heaps." Nor was it single provinces here and there which felt the commotions. The empire itself was rocking to its foundations just previous to the eventful year of 70. There were four emperors within two years, and all of them met with violent deaths. Nero, according to Suetonius, "drove a dagger into his throat"; Galba was run down by several horsemen, and his head was cut off by a common soldier, who, "thrusting his thumb into the mouth," thus carried the horrible trophy; Otho "stabbed himself" in the breast; and Vitellius was despatched by slow torture and then "dragged by a hook into the Tiber." So that it was not now and then a province, but it was, as Suetonius says, "the empire," which was in a "disturbed and unsettled state." Such is the testimony as to the facts by historians who little knew that Christ had foretold all forty years before, when he declared there should be "wars and rumors of wars," nationality arrayed against nationality and king against king, before the end should come, before Jerusalem should be destroyed.

4. Was there anything else to precede this great event? Yes. "Many shall come in my name, saying, I am the Christ; and shall lead many astray." Were there impostors of this kind? Josephus says there was "a great number of false prophets." He mentions one by the name of

Theudas, who persuaded many to "take their effects with them and follow him to the river Jordan," which he was going to "divide"; and, it is added, "many were deluded by his words." We read again in the Jewish historian of an Egyptian who "pretended to be a prophet also, and got together thirty thousand men," whom he promised that from the Mount of Olives he would show "how, at his command, the walls of Jerusalem would fall down." These are only examples of the false Christs, of whom Josephus says there was a "great number," and of whom Christ had prophesied there would be "many." The prediction and the fact accord. There was at the time a feverish expectation very favorable to impostors. Even the pagan Suetonius (and he ought to have known, because he lived in the latter part of the first and the beginning of the second century) says: "A firm persuasion had long prevailed through all the East that it was fated for the empire of the world at that time to devolve on some who should go forth from Judæa." It was because of this prevailing feeling that so many false Christs appeared, and the true Christ foresaw and foretold it all. It was one of the signs which were to precede the overthrow of Jerusalem.

5. Another sign was to be destructive plagues, "great earthquakes," to use Luke's expression, "and in divers places famines and pestilences." Josephus mentions a "famine" in the reign of Claudius so

severe that "many people died for want of what was necessary to procure food." Suetonius refers to a "pestilence" at Rome under Nero, and he says, "within the space of one autumn there died no less than thirty thousand persons." Tacitus speaks of a "failure in the crops, and a famine consequent thereupon." He also states that "frequent earthquakes occurred, by which many houses were thrown down." He alludes to one year wherein "twelve populous cities of Asia fell in ruins from an earthquake"; and he adds, "It is related that immense mountains sank down, that level places were seen to be elevated into hills, and that fires flashed forth during the catastrophe." Josephus describes an earthquake where there were "amazing concussions and bellowings of the earth." Finally, Seneca in the year 58 writes: "How often have cities of Asia and Achæa fallen with one fatal shock! how many cities have been swallowed up in Syria! how many in Macedonia! How often has Cyprus been wasted by this calamity! how often has Paphos become a ruin! News has often been brought us of the demolition of whole cities at once." In the light of such testimony how striking Christ's prediction, "great earthquakes, and in divers places famines and pestilences"!

6. Perhaps the most startling prophecy was that there should be what an evangelist calls "signs in sun and moon and stars," "terrors and great signs from heaven." Were there these? A comet "re-

sembling," says Josephus, "a sword," hung ominously over the city a whole year. One night, according to the same witness, the temple was mysteriously flooded with a light bright as day and lasting "half an hour." On a certain evening just before sunset "chariots and troops of soldiers in their armor were seen running about among the clouds." Stranger than all, the priests one night, on going into the temple to perform their usual duties, "felt a quaking and heard a great noise, and after that they heard a sound as of a multitude, saying, 'Let us remove hence.'" Such are some of the "terrors and great signs from heaven" which Josephus mentions. Tacitus, too, referring to the destruction of Jerusalem, says, "Armies were seen to engage in different parts of the sky; . . . the temple shone by the sudden fire of the clouds; the doors of the temple were suddenly thrown open; a voice, more than human, was heard that the gods were departing, and at the same time a great motion as if departing." Josephus was a Jew, Tacitus was a Roman, and neither was a Christian, but what they write as history Christ had spoken as prophecy.

7. There was one more sign which was to be a precursor of the end: "When ye see Jerusalem compassed with armies, then know that her desolation is at hand. Then let them that are in Judæa flee into the mountains; and let them that are in the midst of her depart out." That was a sign

that the Christians were to make their escape with all haste. Did it turn out as planned for? Four years before the final catastrophe—that is, 66 A. D.—the Roman general Cestius Gallus marched upon Jerusalem, which was in a state of rebellion. He pressed the siege, and had he continued, says Josephus, "a little longer" he would have "certainly taken the city," and would have put "an end to the war that very day." But all at once he beat a retreat. Why? "Without any reason in the world," says the Jewish historian. But there was a reason of which he was ignorant. It was doubtless, in the providence of God, to give the Christians their promised opportunity to escape. Upon the temporary withdrawal of the Romans the city-gates stood open for a while, but in a few days they were closed, and active preparations were carried on so as to resist the siege which was sure to be renewed. Before the blockade, however, "many of the most eminent of the Jews," says Josephus, "swam away from the city, as from a ship when it was going to sink." Among the many we may suppose the Christians to have been. Indeed, Eusebius, the Church historian, who lived from 265 to 340 A. D., expressly says that they "by revelation left the city, and dwelt in a city of Perea, the name of which is Pella." Very soon after this providential escape came the army of Titus, and Jerusalem was destroyed, and also the temple with its goodly stones.

Thus, before the actual destruction there were signs given of the approaching judgment, warnings which the disciples heeded to the advantage of their personal safety. But the vast majority lingered and suffered untold miseries. "They did not," says Josephus, "attend nor give credit to the signs that were so evident." Nor will many now regard the warnings of God. Desolation will some day sweep over them if they do not listen to the voice of mercy which precedes the infliction of punishment. The Lord makes no idle threats; every word of his comes to pass: it did of old, as we have seen, and it will in the future. We need not go down at the last with a sinking world, and yet we shall, as surely as did the ancient Jews, if we do not improve our opportunities. When the last great day of the Lord shall come, the end of the world, of which the destruction of Jerusalem is emblematic—when there shall precede this solemn consummation of human history still more fearful signs than have been considered—may it be ours to be caught up into the air before that final crash and wreck of nature preparatory to the evolving of the new heavens and the new earth. May it be ours to dwell in the New Jerusalem which in the goodness of God succeeds the old.

CHAPTER XIV.

THE BIBLE AND THE DESTRUCTION OF JERUSALEM.

"O Jerusalem, Jerusalem, which killeth the prophets, and stoneth them that are sent unto her! how often would I have gathered thy children together, even as a hen gathereth her chickens under her wings, and ye would not! Behold, your house is left unto you desolate" (MATT. 23:37, 38); "And as he went forth out of the temple, one of his disciples saith unto him, Master, behold, what manner of stones and what manner of buildings! And Jesus said unto him, Seest thou these great buildings? there shall not be left here one stone upon another, which shall not be thrown down" (MARK 13:1, 2); "And when he drew nigh, he saw the city and wept over it, saying, If thou hadst known in this day, even thou, the things which belong unto peace! but now they are hid from thine eyes. For the days shall come upon thee, when thine enemies shall cast up a bank about thee, and compass thee round, and keep thee in on every side, and shall dash thee to the ground, and thy children within thee; and they shall not leave in thee one stone upon another; because thou knewest not the time of thy visitation" (LUKE 19:41, 44); "Then shall be great tribulation, such as hath not been from the beginning of the world until now, no, nor ever shall be" (MATT. 24:21); "And thou shalt eat the fruit of thine own body, the flesh of thy sons and of thy daughters which the Lord thy God hath given thee; in the siege and in the straitness, wherewith thine enemies shall straiten thee" (DEUT. 28:53); "And they shall fall by the edge of the sword, and shall be led captive into all the nations: and Jerusalem shall be trodden down of the Gentiles, until the times of the Gentiles be fulfilled" (LUKE 21:24).

THE destruction of Jerusalem was very positively foretold by Christ some forty years before the event. Nothing seemed more unlikely at the time. The disciples could hardly believe that the predictions would be verified. The city and the temple seemed too substantial and too glorious to be doomed to such utter ruin and desolation. There were three lines of fortification, containing single stones seventy feet in length. The walls were surmounted by strong towers which seemed impregnable. The temple was simply magnificent. There were pillars between thirty and forty feet high, each being an entire stone of white marble, and so large that three men with extended arms were required to reach around one. The gates were plated with gold and they swung on hinges of the same precious metal. The roof was covered with one mass of golden spikes to keep the birds from settling thereon. A golden vine with clusters of grapes and with each bunch as large as a man was the admiration of all. The rabbins said, "Like a true natural vine it grew greater and greater; men would be offering, some gold to make a leaf, some a grape, some a bunch: and these were hung upon it, and so it was increasing continually." Such was the temple, and, says Josephus, at the rising of the sun it "reflected back a very fiery splendor," which forced people to "turn their eyes away, just as they would have done at the sun's own rays"; while at a distance, says this historian, the temple, which he had often seen, appeared "like a mountain covered with snow; for as to those parts of it that were not gilt, they were exceeding white." It is not strange that one of the disciples said admiringly, "Behold, what manner of stones and what manner of buildings." These, however, were not to be left "one stone upon another." It was 70 A. D., under the Roman general Titus, that the catastrophe came. Let us briefly note some of the details of the siege as given in Josephus, Jewish historian of the time and an eye-witness of the successive stages of destruction.

Not the least of the sufferings of the Jews came through the heads of various factions, each striving for the mastery within the doomed walls. The people had once asked for the release of the robber Barabbas in preference to Jesus, and now they were tormented by robber chiefs who with armed bands roamed the streets and plundered and killed, till there was such a reign of terror that the approach of the Romans was actually hailed with delight by the miserable citizens. Titus drew up his legions before the outer wall. His engines and battering-rams began to play. The former threw immense stones, which, flying through the air and shining white in the night, were at first avoided, but when painted black and thus rendered invisible in the darkness, they crushed whole ranks. There was something irresistible in the steady battering of the ram, which was worked backward and forward "by a great multitude of men" with regular swinging strokes. One of the formidable machines, called Niko or Victory because it had never been known to fail, thundered away day and night till a breach was made and the outer wall was taken, and a great part of it was "demolished." The second wall was next attacked. Besiegers and defenders fought desperately until it also succumbed, and Titus "demolished it entirely." Not one stone was left upon another.

Siege was laid to the third wall, and famine began its ravages. "A table," says the Jewish historian, "was nowhere laid for a distinct meal." All ate secretly and hastily, lest their provisions should be discovered and seized by the robbers, who ransacked houses for food, and who, lifting up children, shook them till they let go the morsels to which they clung in their hunger. People would steal out of the city for something to eat, and would be captured by the Romans, and would be crucified to the number of four hundred in one day. They writhed on crosses in sight of fellow-Jews, who crowded the wall above. This tragedy of crucifixion went on till there was actually a scarcity of wood for the making of the transverse beams. "His blood be on us, and on our children!" cried the Jews of Him whom they crucified; and it was, as they also were nailed by the hundreds on crosses.

Meanwhile the progress was slow, the engines and works of assault being skillfully undermined and burned. Titus decided upon another plan of bringing the besieged to terms. He built, we read, "a wall round about the whole city." This was, as another has said, "a military palisade or rampart, made from the earth thrown out of the ditch and stuck with sharp stakes." In three days, the whole army being employed, was the work completed, and when properly garrisoned there was no possibility of ingress or egress; the city could in time be starved into submission. How remarkable that Christ should have foretold this plan of operation forty years before the event!—"The days shall come upon thee, when thine enemies shall cast up a bank [margin, palisade] about thee, and compass thee round, and keep thee in on every side." The Jews were completely hemmed in; "all hope of escaping," says Josephus, "was now cut off, . . . together with their liberty of going out of the city."

The famine became more terrible, whole families being swept off. Houses were full of the dying. In the streets were those who had dropped down dead. The robbers plundered the corpses, and they would laughingly try the edge of their swords upon the naked flesh, and would sometimes thrust through those who "still lay alive upon the ground." For a while the dead were buried, but afterward they were only "cast down from the walls into the valleys beneath." Titus, going his rounds, saw with horror the decaying bodies, whose stench was unendurable, and, groaning aloud, he raised his hands to heaven and "called God to witness that this was not his doing." He seemed half conscious of playing into the hands of an overruling Providence.

The famishing inhabitants stole away from the city in great numbers, and, it becoming known to the enemy that to save their money they swallowed it, the soldiers of Titus set to cutting "open their living bodies" in search of the hidden treasures; and sometimes "pieces of gold" *were* found, but "a great many were destroyed" in the "bare *hope*" of gain. Two thousand were killed in one night for the possible gold they might contain. Though the Roman general threatened his followers with instant death if they continued their horrible work, they still, when detection seemed unlikely, seized Jewish deserters, and, in the words of Josephus, "dissected them and pulled polluted money out of their bowels."

The famine increased till people gnawed old leather. Wisps of hay were eaten, and shoots of trees sold at high prices for food. A wealthy woman of Perea who was caught by the siege in Jerusalem became so maddened with hunger that she slew her nursing child, and, says Josephus, "roasted him and ate the one-half of him, and kept the other half by her concealed" till the robbers, who had plundered her repeatedly, came again. When they came and "threatened her that they would cut her throat immediately if she did not show them what food she had," she replied that she had saved a very fine portion for them, and thereupon she "uncovered what was left of her son." When they refused to eat she reproached them for being more fastidious than a woman; but she was allowed to finish herself the horrid feast, consisting of her own child's flesh. Away back in Deuteronomy it had been prophesied, "Thou shalt eat the fruit of thine own body . . . in the siege and in the straitness, wherewith thine enemies shall straiten thee."

Events fast hurried to a close. Titus called a council to discuss the expediency of destroying the temple, which flames were rapidly approaching. The decision was to save the holy house, and the advancing fire was ordered extinguished. But the Roman soldiers, exasperated by continued Jewish attacks, pressed forward, and one of them, mounting the shoulders of a comrade, contrary to orders applied a blazing torch to a temple window, and the conflagration was started. Titus at the alarm rushed to the scene and commanded the fire to be quenched, but his voice could not be heard in the din and confusion. He signaled with his hand, but every one was too excited to pay any attention. "And thus," says the Jewish historian, "was the holy house burnt down without Cæsar's approbation." It was contrary to the wish of Titus, but it was in accordance with the prediction of Christ, who had said, "Your house is left unto you desolate." The whole structure was ablaze and the fire roared like a volcano. The light was seen for miles. People gathered on the walls of the upper city and sent up their wailings. There was the "shout of the Roman legions," and there was the cry of despair from those "surrounded with fire and sword," while the hills round about returned the echo of the roaring conflagration, the shouting soldiery and the crying multitude.

Zion only remained to be taken, and against its steep cliffs mounds were raised, and soon the battering-rams were thundering away. The Jews were dejected, the Romans confident. A breach was speedily made in the wall; a panic ensued; the people, fleeing hither and thither, were hunted down, and the streets were made to flow with their blood. Orders were given for the demolition of "the entire city and temple." Three massive towers, however, were spared, that future generations might see what "Roman valor had subdued." When Titus examined these he exclaimed, "We have certainly had God for our assistant in this war, . . . for what could the hands of men or any machines do toward overthrowing these towers?" He was right. God had decreed it, and it had been foretold by Christ. Jerusalem was actually "trodden down," and Zion's wall, like the other two, was leveled. "The city," says Josephus, "was so thoroughly laid even with the ground by those that dug it up to the foundation that there was left nothing to make those that came thither believe it had ever been inhabited." Such was the end of a conflict wherein one million one hundred thousand were killed ("and they shall fall by the edge of the sword"), and ninety-seven thousand were taken prisoners and sold, many of them, into slavery ("and shall be led captive into all the nations").

What now had Jesus predicted regarding the destruction of Jerusalem?—"Then shall be great tribulation, such as hath not been from the beginning of the world until now, no, nor ever shall be." What says the Jewish historian in giving a summary of the war?—"It appears to me that the misfortunes of all men from the beginning of the world, if they be compared to those of the Jews, are not so considerable as they were." The fact seems to have corresponded to the prophecy. And what is the judgment of the modern historian? Milman says: "Jerusalem . . . has probably witnessed a far greater portion of human misery than any other spot upon the earth."

A triumph at Rome was voted to Titus for his splendid success. He was crowned with laurel and clothed in purple. His soldiers were arrayed in their finest uniform. The triumphal procession was set in motion amid shouts that rent the air. The tallest and most distinguished of the captured Jews graced the triumph. Carried along in the line of march were beautifully-wrought vessels of

JERUSALEM DESTROYED. 199

silver and gold. There were rarest wild beasts from all quarters of the globe to help make up the display. Ships were borne along in great numbers, and, after the manner of modern transparencies, magnificent pageants three and four stories high whereon was portrayed all the scenery of ancient warfare, such as "a happy country laid waste and entire squadrons of enemies slain," "houses overthrown and falling upon their owners," soldiers pouring through breaches in walls, and other similar scenes drawn true to the facts. Of this grand Roman triumph, decreed for the destruction of Jerusalem, there remains yet a witness in the Arch of Titus, still standing in one of the streets of the Eternal City. On that arch the traveler to-day, after the lapse of centuries, sees represented Jewish captives, the golden candlestick and the triumphal car of the Roman general. For eighteen hundred years that marble arch has been witnessing to the literal fulfillment of God's word. For all these centuries has Jerusalem been "trodden down of the Gentiles."

Three hundred years after the destruction of the city there was a vain attempt by Julian the Apostate to restore the Jewish polity with all the old paraphernalia of worship. This Roman emperor, for the express purpose, says Gibbon, of furnishing an "argument against the faith of prophecy and the truth of revelation," gave orders for the restoration of the temple. From every part of the empire the Jews flocked, and engaged in the work of reconstruction. Rich men labored with spades and pickaxes of silver, and wealthy women carried materials in silk and purple mantles. But the enterprise was strangely interrupted. According to both pagan and Christian writers of the time, when the rubbish had been cleared away and the subterranean caverns had been opened, flames burst from the long-hidden chambers, balls of fire rolled along the ground with thunderous noise, and the workmen had to abandon the undertaking. Whether it was a miraculous interruption of the work in accordance with contemporary belief, or whether it was a natural and not unknown phenomenon of gases long confined exploding on coming in contact with outer air, the work, at any rate, was stopped. The times of the Gentiles had not yet been fulfilled, and Jerusalem had still to be trodden down for at least fifteen hundred years more.

How long the malediction of Heaven against the Holy City is yet to continue in force we cannot say. Whether the Jews shall ever be actually restored to Jerusalem is a question of debate. But that a blessed future is in store for the chosen people upon their conversion to Christ is a part of prophetic teaching. With "the fullness of the Gentiles," says Paul, "all Israel shall be saved." The prophecies of Christ, the predictions of the New Testament and of the Old, have to such an extent been verified that we can well believe in what yet remains unfulfilled of God's word. And there is the bright prospect, if not of an earthly Jerusalem restored, at least of a "new Jerusalem coming down out of heaven from God, made ready as a bride adorned for her husband."

CHAPTER XV.

THE BIBLE AND THE PECULIAR JEWS.

"Lo, it is a people that dwell alone,
And shall not be reckoned among the nations."—Num. 23:9.

THE absolute uniqueness of the Jews as a people is here indicated. They were and are "peculiar," not only in the biblical, but in the modern, sense.

1. The separateness of the Hebrews, predicted in Scripture, has been realized in history. They were to be altogether unlike others, and they have been. They were told just what to eat and what not to eat, their very diet being so prescribed as to make it necessary for them to live by themselves. From the apostles we learn what a holy horror there was among pious Jews of eating meats that had been sacrificed to idols. Matrimonial alliances were forbidden outside of the chosen circle, and even social relations were confined to the strictest lines; to sit at the same table with sinners was a disgrace. How multiform were the ceremonial ablutions to cleanse from any defilement that may have been contracted from coming in contact with the unclean Gentile unawares! This thorough ex-

clusiveness was peculiar to the Jews, and it was of divine ordering. God seems to have had a great plan which could be carried out only by the minutest regulations. The human race was then in its childhood, and had to be governed accordingly. The only mistake, perhaps, of the Jews was their holding on to childish things after they had become men and by various traditions adding to the rules. Still, in a general sense they were true to the plan mapped out for them by God; they were meant to be a peculiar people, clearly marked off from all other nations.

> "Lo, it is a people that dwell alone,
> And shall not be reckoned among the nations."

The result is, that a Jew to this day is a Jew wherever he may be, and all down history he stands out separate and easily recognized. No other nationality can be thus distinctly traced from the beginning down. History opens with Abraham emigrating from "Ur of the Chaldees," and the migratory Jew is still marching on, as unique a character as ever. Whatever the country, whatever the age, the Jew is a Jew—peculiar. This national exclusiveness seems to point to the moulding hand of Him with whom a day is as a thousand years and a thousand years are as a day. Indeed, we can see somewhat of the divine purpose.

2. It seems to us utter folly to worship idols, to

bow before gods innumerable. But polytheism is apparently that to which humanity naturally inclines. Indeed, the ancient world was wholly polytheistic. The very idea of setting apart the Jews was to introduce and spread the doctrine that there is no God except Jehovah; and even the people who were chosen for this mission were themselves so tinctured with the prevailing religious notions as to be constantly going over into idolatry. God had to be severe with them; he had to build walls, insisting upon entire separation and punishing the least intermingling with the heathen, or he could never have established the true doctrine of one God and only One.

Strict as he was, it required centuries to make the Jews themselves thoroughly monotheistic. It was not till the captivity in Babylon that the serving of strange gods was completely rooted out of their hearts. It took two thousand years to get just one nation indoctrinated, for when Christ came the Jews alone were believers in a single Deity pure and simple. The most cultured people on the face of the globe, the educated Greeks, held to "gods many"—so many that in their chief city, Athens, a Roman satirist could say it was easier to find a god than a man.

This, then, is the second great peculiarity of the Jews: their exclusiveness was with a view to educating them into monotheism, and this with the ulterior purpose of bringing all mankind to the worship of one God. It required two thousand years to make one nation believe this doctrine, and nearly two thousand years more have passed away, and still the great majority of the race are idolaters. God understood the gravity of the situation when he set the Jews off by themselves; he saw he must adopt the most stringent measures to overcome polytheism. It is very easy for us to ridicule idolatry, for there have been generations of training back of us; we have inherited the monotheistic doctrine. It is an inheritance which the Jews have given us, and to this source the world is indebted for the passing away of idols.

To be sure, when Mohammedanism swept over three continents almost the very battle-cry was, "There is one God, and Mohammed is his prophet!" but Mohammed borrowed from Moses, and the Koran is an imperfect digest and mutilation of the Old Testament. We think it very peculiar for men to worship idols, whereas the peculiar thing about it is that we are not polytheists instead of worshipers of one God—a peculiarity which has been ground into our very being by the persistent teaching of the Jewish Scriptures. What a power the Jew has been we see when we consider that were it not for his influence we to-day would be bowing down to stocks and stones, or at best to sun, moon and stars! A peculiar people, assuredly, to whom can be traced, under the guidance of God, the overthrow of what is distinctive of heathenism, the debasing worship of material objects. The world is being revolutionized in this respect by Jewish doctrine.

3. Another peculiarity of this people is the idea of a Messiah which they have introduced into history. Renan, the distinguished French skeptical writer, says: "What more than all else characterized the Jew was his confident . . . belief in a brilliant and happy future for humanity." It was the prophet Micah who foretold that out of Bethlehem should proceed a Ruler "whose goings forth are from of old, from everlasting." Away back in Genesis the promise was made to a Jew, "In thy seed shall all the nations of the earth be blessed." How very romantic that orthodox (not rationalizing) Jews are to this day reading the prophecies of a great Deliverer, and are hoping for his coming, or, at least, if not for the coming of a personal Messiah, for the coming of a Messianic kingdom! The result is, their golden age is in their future. Heathen nations look back to the glory of the past, and there is no inspiring hope ahead. The effect is seen in the people's lives; there is nothing to cheer them on, and they sink into a fatalistic view of things; they lose ambition and become dead weights to civilization.

The Jews, however, are expectant; glorious things are in store for them, and they are buoyant and courageous, and there is no likelihood of their dying out, as many another nationality has died.

Flash upon a people the conviction that they are going to make a mark in history, fill them with the thought of a future big with events, and they are ever rousing themselves to realize the pictured ideal. The Jews can never pass out of history so long as the hope of Messiah's reign keeps stirring them to nobler achievements, so long as they are for ever working up to the standard which they are sure will some day be reached. So that this Jewish doctrine of better times to come is lifting mankind into hopefulness, which is the necessary condition to successful development, for a disheartened people never yet accomplished anything. It puts the golden age not behind, but ahead, evermore furnishing a fresh incentive to exertion.

And yet, it may be said, as the Jews number only six or seven (or at most twelve) millions in the whole world, their hope of a Messiah cannot have a very general influence. That is true to a certain extent, but where did Christians get their Messiah? It was Disraeli (was it not?) who said that one half of Christendom worships a Jew, and the other half a Jewess—Jesus and Mary. The irony of this contains some truth. Christianity is of Hebraic origin; salvation is of the Jews, the Master himself said, and to Christianity is due our modern civilization. And while our Christ is in the past so far as his historical environment is concerned, it is the future which is to witness his triumph.

The millennium is yet to be, and all Christendom

feels the thrill of what is to come. Not only actual believers in Christ, but all who have come under the influence of his teaching, are living in expectancy of wondrous developments. To such a height have our expectations risen that we would not be much surprised at anything which might happen. What with railroad and telegraph and telephone and phonograph, what with the springing to new activity wherever the gospel of Christ is known, what with the opening up of countries long unexplored, Christendom is almost wild with expectation. We cannot lie down in sluggishness; the breath of life is blowing over us with a freshness which makes every heart and pulse to bound. Thank God for the Jew, for the Messiah who sprung from the Jew, for that glorious hopefulness which only those nations have that are acquainted with the Messianic kingdom! The gospel has but to touch heathenism and the dry bones begin to stir with life. Japan hears the story and rouses from the sleep of centuries, and is wide awake to enter the race which is to end in victory. Wherever the Jewish Scriptures are read, and only there, is there progress even of the material type, is there a reaching forward for the better things to come; and when we think of it, how our respect for the Jew grows! No other character has been so prominent in the developments which go to make up history, appearing as it does at every turn in the slow unfolding of the divine purpose.

4. There is one characteristic of the Jews as a nation so peculiar that it has made infidels believers —namely, their wide dispersion in exact accordance with prophecy. When Frederick the Great asked his chaplain the strongest argument in a word for the Bible and Christianity, the answer very properly was, "The Jews, Your Majesty."

We read in Deuteronomy, "The Lord shall scatter thee among all peoples, from the one end of the earth even unto the other." Says the same authority, "A byword among all the peoples." "Sifted" is the expression of Amos, "among all the nations." "Wanderers" is the apt description of Hosea. "An hissing and a curse," declares Jeremiah. How literally has it all been fulfilled! The Jews are found everywhere. Missionaries have come across them in China, and even in Central Africa. And a few years ago this paragraph was going the round of the religious press: "Beaconsfield has introduced into Cyprus, among the native troops from India, some Hebrews who claim to be descendants of the mercantile colony .... planted by the navy of Solomon." We could believe almost anything of so romantic, so peculiar a people.

It is no wonder that so much used to be written about "the lost tribes of Israel," supposed to be hidden away somewhere in the earth, while when our American Indians were discovered it was gravely discussed in learned circles if they were not the long-lost tribes, while again some now are maintaining that the Anglo-Saxons are the lost tribes. Still, that word "lost" appears to me altogether inappropriate when applied to a people we could not lose sight of if we tried. There apparently is no country where they do not dwell, "scattered" as they are from pole to pole, "sifted" throughout the world; and it need not be said that they have been "wanderers," giving point to the common phrase, "wandering Jew," and that they have been a "byword" and a "hissing."

Read mediæval history especially, when the Jews had no civil rights, when they were burned by the thousands and when they underwent horrors whose very perusal makes the blood run cold. Read of the more recent Russian atrocities, and of the present race-prejudice against them at Saratoga, where they are excluded from a leading hotel. All down the ages they have been a marked class, and even now, in Webster's latest, we have the definition of "to jew" as to cheat, to swindle. Believers and unbelievers alike have used the term as one of reproach, and so have been verifying prophecy. How can this peculiar accordance between prediction and fact be explained? Is history with its wicked men even in collusion with prophecy to pass a fraud upon the world? Nay, rather men have been unconscious instruments in establishing the word spoken of old by the Lord. What a peculiar people, when not Christians alone, but infidels also, have been playing into God's hands to bring about the fulfillment of prophecies uttered hundreds and thousands of years ago!

5. One more thing with reference to this peculiar people. It is distinctly taught that as a nation they are to be converted to Christ, and even, according to some scholars, restored to Palestine. Zechariah asserts, "They shall look unto me whom they have *pierced*, and they shall mourn." " I will plant them upon their own land," speaks the Lord by Amos, "and they shall no more be plucked up." Jeremiah states, "I will gather you from all the nations, and from all the places whither I have driven you, saith the Lord; and I will bring you again unto the place whence I caused you to be carried away." "I will," says God by Ezekiel, "assemble you out of the countries where ye have been scattered, and I will give you the land of Israel." Though these passages may have had a primary, they certainly have not had a complete, fulfillment; and it must be admitted that they look strongly toward a literal restoration to the Holy Land. Be that as it may (and it is but fair to say that the weight of scholarship seems to be against it), a national *conversion* is predicted without doubt. Paul argues this expressly when he says that with the fullness of the Gentiles "all Israel shall be saved"; and such has been the general belief of the Church. As far back as the year 400, Augustine, the great Latin Father, said, "That in the last times, before the judgment, the Jews (by means

of Elias, who shall expound the law to them) shall believe in Christ, is a thing much asserted in the sayings and hearts of the faithful." In a similar strain the golden-mouthed Chrysostom, the great Greek preacher, spoke; and such has been the faith in all ages.

The Jews are to be converted; they are yet to figure largely in history. What if they are few and far between? what if they do not exceed seven millions in number? It does not require many Jews to count for something. One Jew, and he taken out of prison, ruled Egypt, the richest country of the time. Another Joseph may be born. One Jew, and he a poor captive of war, reigned over Babylon, the most splendid empire of antiquity. Another Daniel may be born. One Jew, and he nailed to a cross, now sways all Christendom, the most extensive kingdom ever founded. With reference to this Jew everything is dated. The infidel recognizes him by the year which he writes at beginning a letter or which he publishes on the title-page of his skeptical book. When a government coins money and when the commercial world transacts business, it is all done in some "year of our *Lord*," who was a Jew. Aside from this most prominent of all Hebrew characters, the Jew still keeps coming up in history with startling conspicuousness, as if to remind mankind that his mission is not yet finished, as if to proclaim that he is still alive and that he means to live. He will not down, any more than Banquo's ghost.

Now he appears as a shining star in the astronomical firmament, Herschel, or as the great Church historian, Neander; again as the profound philosopher, Spinoza or Mendelssohn; once more as the marvelous musician, the grandson Mendelssohn; or as a striking figure in recent French history, Gambetta; or still as the possessor of immense wealth, Rothschild, who through loans to the Turkish government is said to have a practical mortgage on the Holy Land, and who if he has could readily open the way for a literal return of his people to Palestine, and who at least does control the money-market of Europe and of the world; or the conspicuous Jew appears as "the man of destiny" in Beaconsfield, who a few years ago, whether we liked or disliked him, had as England's prime minister more power than any other one person on the face of the globe. No! no! it does not require many Jews to shape history; one can do it, and does do it every now and then, as if to keep our memories stirred up to an appreciation of his splendid capabilities. The British occupancy of Egypt is stated to be "largely in the interest of Jewish capitalists, holders of Egyptian bonds"; and now two Hebrews are even said to have bought the site of ancient Babylon. The Jews thus seem to be getting possession, not only of their own land, but also of the lands of their former oppressors, Egyptian and Babylonian. There is a millennial future for the human race, and the peculiar Jew is to bear a part in the momentous issues out of which shall be evolved the new creation, when all, both Jew and Gentile, shall know the Lord Jesus.

Finally, in the study of such a subject how we are impressed with the fact that Jehovah is from everlasting to everlasting! He is never in a hurry to accomplish his plans. He sits on his throne and controls stupendous movements which extend down the ages. Not only in geological formations, but in spiritual developments, he makes haste slowly. Vast stretches of time are needed to understand God. Away back in the beginning, during the successive steps of evolving order out of chaos, it is recorded, "And God saw that it was good"; and perhaps only he could have seen the good then. When vegetation was so rank that the earth must have seemed one tangled mass of gigantic weeds, only the foreseeing eye of Divinity could have been pleased. "No mere man" could have recognized in the luxuriant growth great beds of coal for keeping teeming populations in the far future warm and comfortable.

We sometimes now are inclined to think that the world is overrun with wickedness, and we query what will come out of the mass of corruption; but God looks on and gives us the quiet assurance that "all things work together for good," and we are to trust him for the verifying of this declaration.

The good time may not come in this generation or in the next or in the next, but we can rest in faith upon Him whose word shall never fail, though the accomplishment may demand cycle upon cycle of time. Through thousands of years he has been carrying the Jews, and he will not relax his purpose till all we who are his peculiar people, who "dwell alone" and are separate from the world, have been brought out of the great tribulation, out of the strife and the conflict, out of sorrow and trial and temptation, out of disappointment and woe, to join in song of praise around the throne in heaven:

"Glory be to the Father, and to the Son, and to the Holy Ghost:
As it was in the beginning, is now, and ever shall be; world without end. Amen."

CHAPTER XVI.

THE BIBLE AND THE MONUMENTS—EGYPT AND ASSYRIA.

"If these shall hold their peace, the stones will cry out."—
LUKE 19 : 40.

WHEN in the triumphal entry of Jesus into Jerusalem the multitudes shouted, "Blessed is the King that cometh in the name of the Lord," the Pharisees wanted the disciples rebuked for their glorification of the Master, who, however, replied, "If these shall hold their peace, the stones will cry out." Numerous have been the defences of the Bible, and they are constantly multiplying. Christ has still many enthusiastic followers who are exalting his name and his word. My voice has been lifted up to assist in swelling the hallelujah chorus. How can one keep silent? Who would not like to be able to set forth the truth with greater power? There is appreciation of Antony's feeling when he said that had he the eloquence of Brutus, he would make

"The stones of Rome to rise in mutiny."

God, in this century of most aggressive attack upon

the Scriptures, has put lips in the inanimate, as we shall see by a consideration of the Bible and the monuments.

The nature of this particular kind of Scripture verification has already been foreshadowed by references to the Moabite Stone and the Nabonnedus Cylinder, the signets of Haggai and Jeremiah, the actual unearthing of Pithom, one of the store-cities built by the Hebrew slaves, and the statues and massive works and tombs of the Pharaohs. The growing importance of this line of evidences in the excavations which are being so diligently prosecuted in lands covered or touched by scriptural story would seem to make advisable a separate and distinct treatment of this interesting phase of the subject. Whole volumes are being written upon this special department of biblical study, and within the space at our command we can only glance at the striking facts, while yet the whole ground will be substantially covered. The apparent discrepancies in the two records, written and monumental, will doubtless continue to disappear as inscriptions are deciphered. For our present purpose of simply opening up this boundless field of investigation it is sufficient to note the positive confirmations being given by the very stones to the holy oracles. The ancients, who would have least desired to establish the sacred writings of the Hebrews, are preaching to us, in a more real sense than Shakespeare had in mind, "sermons in stones."

1. Egypt is yielding up her secrets. Her monuments have ever been impressive. Her pyramids and obelisks have been the wonder of the world. Even the ruins of her mighty temples are of astonishing beauty. Of the mass of material thus put at our disposal, while the pickaxe of the excavator is ever disclosing more, we shall have to be content to use but a small part.

Fifteen hundred years before the Christian era Amenophis III. erected near Thebes, on the banks of the Nile, two colossal statues, originally with their crowns about seventy feet in height, which, now uncrowned, are still sitting in majestic repose where they were first located. One of these has been famous in history as "vocal Memnon," which was long said to emit at daybreak a harp-like sound. This fabled music, which has been the inspiration of poets ever since, may not have been, after all, a mythological fancy, but a natural and actual phenomenon, for certain cooled stones now, on receiving the warming rays of the morning sun, are said to crackle or vibrate with a melody not unlike that resulting from the breaking of a harp-string. Indeed, all the statues of Egypt have become vocal since we have learned in the present century to read the inscriptions thereon.

The Egyptian hieroglyphics long baffled the best modern scholarship. The strange alphabet, which consisted of animals and birds with such intervening marks as children might make, was for centuries wholly enigmatical. The knowledge of the mysterious characters had perished from the earth. What eager desire there was to read the secrets which the unknown syllabary was believed to contain! Would there ever be a successful decipherer? At this stage of the problem there came a providential discovery. In 1799 a French officer was excavating for a building near the mouth of the Rosetta branch of the Nile, when he found what is known as the Rosetta Stone, now safely resting in the British Museum. This is a slab of black marble a little over three feet high, nearly two feet and a half wide and ten inches thick. It contained an inscription of one of the Ptolemies, and the date was about 195 B. C. Fortunately, the recorded decree was in three languages—hieroglyphic, cursive Egyptian and Greek. The last, being well understood, gave a key to the unknown tongues, and in course of time, under the patient labors of various scholars, the hieroglyphics became intelligible, and the results reached were confirmed by the knowledge gained from a second trilingual inscription (that of San), brought to light in 1866. This dated still farther back, to 238 B. C., and the hieroglyphic portion was more complete than on the Rosetta Stone. Thus, when human learning stood dumb and wondering before the Egyptian hieroglyphics, Providence came to the aid of scholars by revealing stones brought forth from their hiding-places. The inanimate rock became animate;

it spoke out, and opened the way for the reading of the monuments, to which we will now listen.

On the site of old and once proud Thebes is a massive pile, at present known as the temple of Karnak, which covers five times as much ground as St. Paul's in London, and which occupies more than twice as much space as St. Peter's at Rome. On its walls are sculptured inscriptions which with our recently acquired knowledge we can read. Now, there is a scriptural record like this: "And it came to pass in the fifth year of King Rehoboam that Shishak king of Egypt came up against Jerusalem." Is there any monumental confirmation of this statement? On that very temple of Karnak, about one thousand years before Christ, Shishak (or Sheshonk) I. inscribed in stone an account of a successful military expedition of his, and among his conquests he expressly names the "kingdom of Judah," or "Judah-king," besides several familiar points in Palestine.

These direct agreements of scriptural and monumental history are numerous, and let me next call attention to a more indirect example of harmony, for confessedly the more subtle proofs are the stronger. When witnesses agree without design, and without its appearing on the face of the testimony that they were coming to the same point, the result thus reached is irresistibly conclusive, because there is evidently no collusion.

In the second book of the Kings we read of the

Syrians saying, "Lo, the king of Israel hath hired against us the kings of the Hittites and the kings of the Egyptians." A critic of the Bible not many years ago referred to the "unhistorical" character of this passage, because the insignificant Hittites were ranged right along with the Egyptians, a great and powerful people. But were the Hittites so unimportant? Most of us have been accustomed to think of them as we would of a petty tribe of Indians, like the Cherokees or Choctaws. But there are various biblical intimations that they once played a leading part on the world's stage of action. Therefore the Bible, such has been the claim, is to be discredited. To be sure, Uriah was a Hittite, and his wife Bathsheba became the mother of Solomon and an ancestress of Christ; but, after all, did the Hittites ever occupy a prominent place in history? It has been learned in the last few years that they did. Anciently they contested the supremacy of the East not only with Assyria, but also with Egypt. In the long struggle with the latter country, when it was in its prime under Rameses the Great, the king of the Hittites could finally treat with the great Pharaoh on equal terms, and their treaty of peace we have graven in stone on the wall of the temple at Karnak. The parties named are the "great king of Kheta" and the "great prince of Egypt." The inscription professes to be a copy of the terms proposed by the former, who had them written on a "silver tablet," whose contents the latter had chiseled in stone upon his finest temple. The proposition in general was thus stated: "From this very day forward, that there may subsist a good friendship and a good understanding." It was an alliance offensive and defensive, and it was made in 1354 B. C. Thus the very stones at Karnak cry out to the greatness of the Hittite empire, to which the Scriptures by implication witness.

Nor is this all: other stones show that the Hittites formerly extended their sway from the Euphrates on the east to the Ægean Sea on the west. This has been curiously determined within the last dozen years, and the following of the thread which has restored a "forgotten empire" to history is not without interest. The pass of Karabel is a narrow defile in the ancient road connecting Ephesus on the south with Sardis and Smyrna on the north. Herodotus wrote that Sesostris, who was Rameses of Egypt, left memorials of himself in the pass—namely, "two images cut by him in the rock;" "on either side a man is carved." These having been seen in the present century, Professor Sayce of Oxford decided to go and give them a careful examination. He was incited to this by the finding of stones in Hamath whose hieroglyphics were believed to be of Hittite origin, and especially since there were later discoveries of similar inscriptions at Carchemish, the great Hittite capital on the banks of the Euphrates. Rock-statues and stones, with the same unknown characters, kept coming to light here and there. The Oxford scholar had an idea that the figures in the pass of Karabel, which Herodotus had thought to be of Egyptian origin, were really Hittite remains. To determine what the fact was, he visited the pass in 1879, and he ascertained that one of the sculptured warriors did have the same hieroglyphics as appeared in the other Hittite inscriptions, while the style of art was likewise Hittite. The second figure was defaced, but was evidently the companion-piece described by the Greek historian twenty-three centuries ago.

Then not far from Karabel is another monument of Hittite art. In the high cliffs of Sipylus there is carved in the living rock a woman, and since, when rain runs down over the stone figure, there is the appearance of tears being shed by the statue, the Greeks naturally saw in the sitting goddess their weeping Niobe turned to stone. Homer had spoken of her mourning over the loss of her twelve children till she was petrified — "transformed to stone," said the blind bard, "mid the rocks and desert hills of Sipylus." But both Herodotus and Homer were mistaken in their identification of the figures in the Karabel Pass and on Mount Sipylus with Egyptian and Grecian hero and heroine, as Hittite characters at both places prove. The fond dreams of the cultured Greeks must be shattered in these latter days, and were they to come to life we could only say comfortingly, Be not over your loss, "like Niobe, all tears." Those Hittite monuments from the Euphrates clear across Asia Minor show, equally with the sculptured treaty with Rameses at Karnak, how extensive must have been the kingdom of the Hittites, who have been resuscitated from an oblivion of centuries by the speaking of long dumb stones.

The rocky lips are yet silent in one respect. The strange script on Hittite remains has not yet been satisfactorily deciphered, but Professor Sayce believes "the mute stones will yet be taught to speak" when more monuments have been disinterred, and when perhaps there shall be discovered some bilingual or trilingual text to help in the decipherment. Further explorations among buried cities may yet reveal a key to the mysterious Hittite tongue, of which the value of a few characters has been ascertained from a brief solitary bilingual inscription of the first century on a silver boss now lost, though not till its impression had been secured. Since Rameses married the daughter of the Hittite monarch in order to cement the famous treaty they made, if her body should ever be found, as the mummy of her royal husband has been exhumed, possibly, as another has suggested, there may be with her remains the "silver tablet" from which the inscription at Karnak was copied in stone thirteen and a half centuries before Christ. Or this metallic plate, on whose surface the characters were hammered from the reverse side, may be hanging in the sepulchral vault of the father of Pharaoh's bride, in the subterranean tomb of him who had the silver tablet inscribed. But the stones have already spoken with sufficient distinctness to justify the sacred writer in the coupling as equals of "the kings of the Hittites and the kings of the Egyptians."

As to late results of Egyptian explorations, a most remarkable discovery should have a passing notice. An early monarch (Khunaten, or Amenophis IV.) removed his capital from Thebes to a point north thereof, at Tell el-Amarna, to which he transferred the national archives, placing them in the palace library there. These were uncovered in 1887, and hundreds of clay tablets inscribed with Babylonian characters, the court language of the time, have appeared. They contain official communications from surrounding peoples to the rulers of Egypt. There are despatches from the governor of Jerusalem itself, as well as from the farther East. These show that historic records in alphabetic form were common in the fifteenth century before Christ; that is, before the Exodus and before the time of Moses. There is thus overthrown at one stroke a strong position of the skepticism which has been claiming that the reputed author of the Pentateuch is not to be credited, because there were only unreliable traditions which could have been used, there having been no written documents at so remote a period. That single archæological revelation in Upper Egypt utterly sweeps away a great mass of learned infidel arguments directed against the authenticity and trustworthiness of the Mosaic books. Before Moses was, were written these tablets, which prove that there was an active literary correspondence carried on so long ago throughout the Orient. The stones make short work of much high-sounding criticism.

2. Turning next to Assyria, its secrets could be disclosed only by the mastery of another language, more mysterious, if anything, than the Egyptian hieroglyphics. There were strange arrow-headed characters that seemed incapable of being deciphered. And yet a cuneiform literature, representing a spoken tongue of remote antiquity, was rising from the dust of ages. The books of distant centuries were constantly being exhumed—volumes not written with pen and ink on perishable paper, but consisting of plastic clay which had been cut with a metal stylus, and which had been afterward dried in the sun or baked with fire. The clayey material was wrought into bricks, that, suitably inscribed, were laid in magnificent buildings, or into tablets that graced various niches, or into prisms and cylinders which were often pierced through the centre as if for mounting, so as to be read by turning the successive sides to the student. Vast numbers of these books in stone have been gathered from Oriental ruins within the present

century, till the Assyrian literature thus collected already comprises more than the whole Old Testament, and is steadily increasing in bulk. We do not know what may yet be brought to light—perhaps that tablet upon which Ezekiel speaks of having made pictorial impressions with prophetic intimations. In strict accordance with the custom of the age and its people, the prophet says that when he was a captive "in the land of the Chaldeans" he received this divine command: "Take thee a tile and lay it before thee, and portray upon it a city, even Jerusalem; and lay siege against it, and build forts against it, and cast up a mount against it; set camps also against it, and plant battering-rams against it round about." It was soft clay which he was thus to manipulate in order to teach an important lesson, to furnish "a sign to the house of Israel." This little incident shows that Ezekiel was really among those Eastern people—that he was an historic person. And whether his impressed clay is ever discovered or not, there certainly are most remarkable discoveries being made along this very line.

In the excavations at Nineveh a whole library has been dug from the ruins. The royal collection of Assurbanipal, the Sardanapalus of the Greeks, after having been buried for twenty-five hundred years, has been opened to the public. It was no small library, either, with its thousands of tablets and fragments thereof. But how were the cuneiform characters of these books ever read in these our own times? They required long and close study. There would be inscriptions which would begin in the same way, with the exception of one word. The thought occurred that this varying word was the name of the monarch, which of course was changed from time to time, while the royal titles remained the same. Every sovereign of England since Henry VIII. has been called "Defender of the Faith," and one unacquainted with English would see that title again and again in the list of British rulers, whose names would yet be ever varying from Henry to Victoria. An acute observer noticed something similar to this in Assyrian annals. Then with the aid of his knowledge of history he experimented. He would guess that certain arrow-headed marks stood for Darius, of whom he had learned through Greek sources. Going forward, he would try Xerxes for the same number of cuneiform characters. That worked all right for his conjectural theory, since the equivalent of the letter r in each name came just in the right place. Descending the line, Artaxerxes should be the same as Xerxes with a prefix, and it was even so. Thus a clue was gotten to a successful decipherment.

Then there came in a stone to help. The patriarch Job once said:

> "Oh that my words were now written!
> Oh that they were inscribed in a book!
> That with an iron pen and lead
> They were graven in the rock for ever!"

The Persian monarch Darius did just such writing. On the now famous Rock of Behistun, within his ancient realm, he made a trilingual inscription. The face of the rock he smoothed with great care, and at an elevation which must have rendered ladders or scaffolding necessary he wrote with a pen of iron in imperishable stone that which we can read after the lapse of nearly two and a half millenniums. The inscription is in three languages, Persian, Median and Babylonian, and the comparisons which could thus be instituted helped to fix the values of the arrow-headed characters, and by patient toil a lost tongue has been recovered.

The world was amazed and even skeptical, but to test the accuracy of the renderings an inscribed cylinder would be given to two and three experts, and a committee examining the results, arrived at separately and independently, found there was substantial agreement, and doubts could be entertained no longer. The Rock of Behistun played an important part in getting at the meaning of the cuneiform characters; the stone cried out its assistance in the mastering of a language whose literature was so strongly to confirm the Bible. Well did Darius include in his long inscription this appeal to the future observer: "Thou, who shalt hereafter see this tablet which I have written, and these figures, destroy them not." The inscription in these far subsequent times has turned out to be much more important than even Darius could have imagined.

What, then, are some of the confirmations which Scripture receives from the tablets and cylinders of Assyria? They give an account of creation closely resembling the narrative in Genesis. They tell us of a great deluge like the Biblical Flood, and while Assyria and Babylonia looked at this catastrophe from the polytheistic point of view, rather than from the monotheistic standpoint of Scripture, the same original event is manifestly described. Listen to what the ancient monuments say: "Build the ship, save what thou canst of the germ of life;" "bitumen I poured over the outside," "bitumen I poured over the inside;" "bid the seed of life of every kind mount in the midst of the ship;" "the deluge of Rimmon reaches unto heaven;" "like reeds the corpses floated;" "I sent forth a dove," "and it came back;" "I sent forth a swallow," "and it came back;" "I sent forth a raven," "it did not return;" "in the mountain of Nizir stopped the ship;" "I built an altar on the peak of the mountain;" "the great goddess at her approach lighted up the rainbow." Such are detached sentences from what was written on clay and placed in royal libraries twenty-five hundred years ago, and we to-day can read the wedge-shaped inscriptions on baked tablets that have risen from the graves of a dim and remote past. The very stones are crying out that a primeval flood is no Biblical myth.

We read much in Scripture regarding the king of

Assyria who under various names had a part in shaping the history of the Hebrew monarchy from time to time. There is Shalmaneser II., who has left his own records graven in stone. He came to the Assyrian throne 858 B. C. He marched eastward and inscribed his victories on the rocks of Armenia, and there with pen of iron were traced these words concerning those he overthrew: "Ten thousand men belonging to Ahab of Israel." Then a small obelisk of black marble, giving the annals of this same Shalmaneser, now stands in the British Museum, and upon it we read of the subjugation of another Israelitish king, who is expressly named "Jehu," whose ambassadors are represented in relief as bringing tribute, and the peculiar features which still characterize the Hebrew race are easily recognizable.

We read in Isaiah of the capture of "Ashdod" by "Sargon the king of Assyria." For twenty-five centuries this passage of Scripture was the sole witness we had that there was such an Assyrian monarch, but among the recent discoveries is the fragment of a cylinder bearing the name of this very king, Sargon, and giving a description of the identical expedition to the Mediterranean sea-coast mentioned by the prophet; while also his existence clears up difficulties connected with the tenth and eleventh chapters of Isaiah, which did not apply to any known conqueror.

Coupled in scriptural and monumental story are

Sennacherib and Hezekiah. The sacred record reads: "Hezekiah king of Judah sent to the king of Assyria to Lachish, saying, I have offended; return from me: that which thou puttest on me will I bear." That the Assyrian monarch was at that city in his approach to Jerusalem is indicated by a sculptured scene now in London, with the inscription, "Sennacherib, the king of multitudes, the king of Assyria, sat on an upright throne, and the spoil of the city of Lachish passed before him." So, again, the inspired penman says: "In the fourteenth year of King Hezekiah did Sennacherib king of Assyria come up against all the fenced cities of Judah, and took them." On winged and human-headed bulls, which we have, Sennacherib inscribed, "As for Hezekiah of Judah, who had not submitted to my yoke, forty-six of his strong cities . . . I captured. . . . Hezekiah himself I shut up like a bird in a cage in Jerusalem, his royal city." The Bible also says of this Assyrian, "When he was come into the house of his god, they that came forth of his own bowels slew him there with the sword." The reason for his being slain by his elder sons seems to have been because he favored a younger brother of theirs for his successor; and of this favoritism there is a curious confirmation in a preserved tablet whereon is inscribed Sennacherib's will bequeathing to Esarhaddon "armlets of gold, quantities of ivory," and there follows a long list of "beautiful things."

Scripture says he was murdered by his own sons, and a monument gives us the probable reason in a record of very manifest partiality for one specially-named child. Thus do the stones cry out in defence of Biblical history.

When the royal favorite ascended the Assyrian throne he likewise made tributary to him several kings, among whom he names on a cylinder "Manasseh king of Judah." This accords with the sacred record, which says of Esar-haddon that he "took Manasseh in chains, and bound him with fetters." There is added, however, in the book of Chronicles a statement which long troubled commentators—namely, the expression "and carried him to Babylon." Why should it not have been to Nineveh, which was the Assyrian capital? Here, many used to think, is an inaccuracy showing the unhistorical character of the Chronicles. It was as if in the far future some one should read of the present that Queen Victoria conquered India and brought its princes to Paris. Such seemed to be the biblical mistake. But now the monuments tell us that Esar-haddon repaired Babylon and made it one of his seats of government, so that we have an easy explanation of the scriptural record, upon a fuller knowledge of the past. One ignorant of our own early history, if he should read that the governor of Connecticut once conveyed a prisoner of war to the capital at New Haven, might suppose the historian had erred, for according to the present fact Hartford is the capital of that State. But let him learn a little more, and he finds that Connecticut formerly had two capitals, Hartford and New Haven, and the alleged inaccuracy becomes a subtle proof of truthfulness. The stones in these later times have cried out in defence of the absolute accuracy of the divine chronicler, who had written that Manasseh was carried "to Babylon."

The glory of the Assyrian empire culminated with Assurbanipal, who collected the magnificent library from whose pages, written with iron pen in the rock for ever, we have been largely gleaning for our present fund of information. His kingdom survived him only a short time. The whole mighty fabric toppled in shapeless ruins, in which (606 or 610 B. C.) was involved the splendid capital Nineveh, that "great city" wherein, said the prophet Jonah, were more than one hundred and twenty thousand persons who could not "discern between their right hand and their left." Its destruction had been predicted by Nahum, while Zephaniah had prophesied, "How is she become a desolation, a place for beasts to lie down in!" Never was prediction more terribly fulfilled, for the very site of Nineveh was forgotten till it was revealed by the excavations of this nineteenth century. God had a purpose in hiding her beneath the accumulations of ages. When in our day infidelity has become rampant, when the Old Testament has with great confidence been pronounced a mass of fables, the very stones have risen from the ground to verify in baked brick and tablet and rock and cylinder what of the sacred records had been fiercely assailed by a skeptical criticism.

CHAPTER XVII.

THE BIBLE AND THE MONUMENTS.—BABYLONIA AND PALESTINE.

"If these shall hold their peace, the stones will cry out."—
Luke 19 : 40.

IN the continued consideration of the Bible and the monuments we pass to another Oriental country.

3. Babylonia next claims our attention. This was an older empire than the Assyrian, but it had perished, to rise again from the ashes of its younger competitor. Excavations at Babylon have not yet proceeded so far as at Nineveh, but more and more of its stones are crying out. There are here cuneiform inscriptions evidently referring to what in Scripture is known as the tower of Babel with its confusion of tongues. We can read in wedge-shaped letters of a "mound" destroyed in a night, while Anu "confounded great and small on the mound" and "made strange their counsel."

The prophet Habakkuk had said of Babylon, "The stone shall cry out of the wall, and the beam out of the timber shall answer it;" and this has come to pass in the identification of the resplendent palace of Nebuchadnezzar with the modern ruin called Kasr, wherein almost every brick is inscribed with that celebrated monarch's name. He wanted to crush the people of God, but if he had known that in the far future he was to assist in the establishing of their sacred writings, he might well have uttered the prayer of Macbeth, when before the murder of Duncan he, according to our great English dramatist, thus besought the earth:

"Hear not my steps, which way they walk, for fear
The very stones prate of my whereabout."

He did not intend to confirm Ezekiel in one of the latter's allusions, but he did unconsciously. The prophet in speaking of Damascus had associated the city "with the wine of Helbon." Singularly enough, in one of Nebuchadnezzar's expeditions to the Mediterranean, as he marched from Damascus toward the sea along the gorge of the Dog River, he wrote on the face of a cliff an inscription which only recently was discovered under a mass of shrubbery and maiden-hair fern; and what was it that he wrote with iron pen in the rock for ever? Simply a list of the wines of Lebanon, among which the wine of Helbon near Damascus is prominent. Rock-inscription of Babylonian monarch and written prophecy of inspired penman are mutually corroborative.

In the case of Cyrus, too, there is a wonderful agreement between the Scriptures and the monuments. Among the late discoveries are clay documents which revolutionize previous ideas concerning this ancient ruler. He has generally been supposed to have been a Persian monotheist, but by these contemporary records in stone he appears as an Elamite polytheist, and Isaiah is thus seen to have spoken with the greatest exactness when he said of the coming attack upon Babylon: "Go up, O Elam; besiege, O Media," wherein Elam has been explained to mean Persia. No such wrong explanation is now needed, for a forced harmony is no longer necessary in the interest of supposed truth. Then the monumental representation of Cyrus as a "worshiper" of Merodach and other gods agrees better with Scripture than the theory which many have been holding, that he was a Zoroastrian believer in a single deity, and therefore was prepared to sympathize with the Jews in his restoration of them to their native land. The prophet says explicitly, "I will gird thee, though thou hast not known me;" and of course he had not known Jehovah when he tells us in the cylinder of his own writing how he worshiped the Babylonian divinities. He may indeed have been sympathetic toward the Hebrew belief in one God, because of the knowledge he had of monotheism through Persia, where he informs us his great-grandfather had reigned. It is possible also, as Josephus asserts, that he read Isaiah's prophecy which referred to him by name, and that he became a believer in Jehovah, but certainly this was not true at first, for

God is represented as saying "I have surnamed thee, though thou hast not known me." He may have restored the Jews to Palestine because of his political sagacity. He may have seen the danger of keeping a disaffected people in the centre of his realm, and he may have sought their friendship by allowing them to return to their own land, and he may have seen the practical wisdom of buttressing his empire by letting them as friends build up their own institutions on the Egyptian frontier, rather than have them as enemies in the heart of his kingdom to poison other minds with rebellious feelings. But even in this view of the matter God overruled all for the accomplishment of his own divine purpose relative to the chosen people; he made use of an unconscious instrument, as Holy Writ declares.

The further harmony between Isaiah's prophecy and the cylinder of Cyrus appears when in the former we read, "the gates shall not be shut," pointing to a peaceful conquest of the golden city, and when in the latter we read, "I entered Babylon in peace," "without fighting or battle." Likewise, the noble character ascribed to Cyrus by Xenophon and Herodotus, who make him the model prince of antiquity, and implied in the scriptural references, "I have raised him up in righteousness," "he is my shepherd, and shall perform all my pleasure,"— this characterization from profane and sacred sources is almost a repetition of what the cylinder says: "He governed in justice," "righteous in hand and heart," "the nobles and priests who had revolted kissed his feet, they rejoiced in his sovereignty, their faces shone." Then as to the biblical statement that he restored the Jews to the Holy Land, the cylinder implies as much when it says of the various provinces whose inhabitants were in the Babylonian captivity, "All their peoples I assembled, and I restored their lands." Thus do the stones cry out to the truthfulness of what the Bible says concerning Cyrus the Great.

Of Darius, the son of Hystaspes, whether he be the one who captured Babylon by the stratagem of diverting the Euphrates from its bed, whether he thus took the city by surprise or not, he at any rate records two conquests of it in his inscription on the Rock of Behistun, and one of these may have been the familiar event to which the Greek writers refer, for he did not write fully, since he himself says, "Much else has been done by me which is not written in this inscription. For this reason it is not written, that it may not seem too much to him who hereafter reads this inscription, that he may not disbelieve what I have done, may not consider it a lie." Very good advice that is from the Rock of Behistun; it is the stone crying out not to make too much of omissions, and to remember that all ancient history is fragmentary.

4. Having hastily traversed Egypt, Assyria and Babylonia, we come lastly to Palestine, and partic-

ularly to the results of recent explorations on the temple-hill at Jerusalem.

The book of the Kings tells us of the great and hewed stones laid in the temple of Solomon with the co-operation of Hiram of Tyre. Eighty feet below the present surface of the earth has been uncovered massive masonry whereon are marks which have been recognized as Phœnician characters. The corner-stone itself of that unequaled house of God is believed to have been found in a granite block fourteen feet long and imbedded in the solid rock, and which has been dressed to fit its present place. Near by also, in a hole cut in the native rock, has been discovered a small earthenware jar which may have contained the consecrating oil used in the joyful and solemn service of dedication three thousand years ago.

The Pool of Siloam has for all biblically informed a romantic interest. Solomon, according to the book of Ecclesiastes, says, "I made me pools of water." We know that this king of splendid name did give his attention to a proper water-supply for Jerusalem, and Siloam in its initial state may have been due to his enterprise. It was Hezekiah, however, who really brought the work to perfection, and who perhaps is to be credited with its entire construction. We read in the inspired chronicle that this Jewish king at the threatening approach of Sennacherib "took counsel with his princes and his mighty men to stop the waters of the fountains which were without the city;" and the result of the conference was that "they stopped all the fountains, and the brook that flowed through the midst of the land, saying, Why should the kings of Assyria come, and find much water?" That is, the purpose was to divert the water which was without to some point within the city. This seems to have been done, for we read farther in the Chronicles, "This same Hezekiah also stopped the upper spring of the waters of Gihon, and brought them straight down on the west side of the city of David." There is at present only one perennial spring in close proximity to Jerusalem, and that is the Virgin's Fountain. This flows through a tunnel cut in the rock and under the hill to what is still known as the Pool of Siloam. Different persons have gone the entire length of the subterranean channel, which winds along its underground way for one-third of a mile. Sometimes one can stand in the excavated canal; again he has to creep, and at one point he has to crawl. This tunnel is believed to date back to Hezekiah, if not to Solomon. The Pool of Siloam was thus supplied from a living spring, whose waters, Isaiah says, flowed "softly." The receptacle which caught the gurgling stream was famous. Christ called attention to a tower of Siloam falling and crushing eighteen persons. He directed a blind man to go there to wash, while it is said that the pool by interpretation meant Sent, and the waters were sent there, whereas naturally they would have flowed off down the valley. It was water from Siloam, borne in golden vessels to the temple by a triumphal procession on the great day of the feast of tabernacles, which is thought by some to have suggested the Lord's words when he "stood and cried, saying, If any man thirst, let him come unto me, and drink." Very precious, therefore, are the associations of Siloam. An oft-sung hymn says,

"By cool Siloam's shady rill,"

and a modern traveler speaks of listening to the "music of the waters" as he stood in the underground channel "sheltered from the fierce rays of the midday sun."

In the summer of 1880 some boys were making their way up the rock-cut canal, when one of them slipped and fell. Upon rising from the water he noticed what seemed to be letters on the wall of the stone passage. He reported what he had seen, and a careful examination by experts disclosed an ancient inscription, largely under water, on an artificial tablet. The form of letters is that used eight centuries before Christ, and the opinion of scholars is that we have what was written by order of Hezekiah at the completion of the great work. And how does the inscription read?—"Now this is the history of the excavation. While the excavators were still lifting up the pick, each toward his neighbor, and while there were yet three cubits to (excavate, there was heard) the voice of one man calling to his neighbor." The vivid description continues, that when "the excavators had struck pick against pick, one against the other, the waters flowed from the spring to the pool."

We thus learn from the very stones all about the construction of the tunnel, which is seen to have been begun simultaneously at each end, with the workmen to meet in the middle; and so skillful was mechanical engineering even at that remote time that the laborers, notwithstanding the serpentine course of the passage, came almost face to face at the centre, striking pick to pick, while they shouted to each other through the thin partition, till they actually met with an enthusiasm which could not be repressed, and which to-day, after the lapse of more than twenty-five hundred years, becomes almost vocal through the rocky inscription. The stone literally cries out, and confirms what the chronicler had said of Hezekiah, and what the book of the Kings relates regarding him: "He made the pool, and the conduit, and brought water into the city."

We come lastly to the temple of Herod. Its greatest glory arises from its connection with Christ. Could we have a relic from that sacred building, which the Lord repeatedly entered, and which his disciples so greatly admired when he prophesied that one stone should not be left upon another, we might consider ourselves supremely favored. This structure was also closely related to more than one event in the lives of the apostles. There, for instance, is that stirring scene in the career of Paul when he was thought to have desecrated the edifice by taking with him a Gentile into its inner precincts. He was saved from an enraged Jewish mob only by Roman soldiers. Why were the excited people "seeking to kill him"? The narrative in the book of the Acts replies: "For they had before seen with him in the city Trophimus the Ephesian, whom they supposed that Paul had brought into the temple." Was the court of the Israelites thus jealously guarded against all aliens from their commonwealth? Josephus answers: "When you went through these first cloisters into the second court of the temple, there was a partition made of stone all around, whose height was three cubits: its construction was very elegant; upon it stood pillars at equal distances from one another, declaring the law of purity, some in Greek and some in Latin letters, that no foreigner should go within that sanctuary." The Jewish historian also represents Titus as speaking of "this partition-wall before your sanctuary," while this Roman conqueror of the holy city adds, "Have you not been allowed to put up the pillars thereto belonging at due distances, and on it to engrave in Greek and in your own letters this prohibition, that no foreigner should go beyond this wall? Have not we given you leave to kill such as go beyond it, though he were a Roman?"

Paul must have been familiar with that dividing wall, and he would have been able to read the Greek inscription on the pillars, for it was on this occasion of which we are treating that the chief captain, on hearing his request for permission to say a word, asked, " Dost thou know Greek ?" He had supposed the apostle to be the well-known seditious Egyptian, until he heard in Greek the apostolic request for liberty to speak to the excited throng. So that Paul understood all about that stone wall of separation between Jews and Gentiles, and all about that Greek inscription on the surmounting pillars. And when he nearly lost his life because he was supposed to have taken Trophimus of Ephesus beyond the plainly-indicated dividing-line, still more would he have occasion to remember the cause of all his trouble. Of course the Ephesians also would hear of the whole matter through Trophimus, who was from Ephesus. In view of all this, the entire authenticity, or at least the especial pertinency, of Paul's Epistle to the Ephesians is shown by nothing more than by that single expression occurring in this very letter—namely, that Christ "brake down the middle wall of partition."

The climax of this striking line of evidence is yet to be mentioned. In 1871 the excavations at Jerusalem revealed a stone with this Greek inscription : " No foreigner to proceed within the partition wall and enclosure around the sanctuary ; whoever is caught in the same will on that account be liable to incur death." This is reliably pronounced to be one of the very inscribed pillars which Josephus and Titus mention, which Christ and Paul must have often read, which Trophimus and the Ephesians must have thought of when they received their letter from the chief of the apostles containing a reference to the "middle wall of partition." This is testimony that is fairly dramatic in its culminating force. It is the crying out of the very stones, which have actually sent forth one of their number from the rubbish of eighteen centuries to stand up and talk to this generation in the Greek of the first century.

We cannot conclude better than in the language of an accomplished Oxford professor (Sayce), who says: "The same spirit of skepticism which had rejected the early legends of Greece and Rome had laid its hands also on the Old Testament, and had determined that the sacred histories themselves were but a collection of myths and fables. But suddenly, as with the wand of a magician, the ancient Eastern world has been reawakened to life by the spade of the explorer and the patient skill of the decipherer, and we now find ourselves in the presence of monuments which bear the names or recount the deeds of the heroes of Scripture. One by one these 'stones crying out' have been examined or more perfectly explained, while others of equal importance are being continually added." If, then, any have been inclined to give up God's word because of the confident assaults made upon it by an unbelieving criticism; if their faith has been so far weakened that, instead of being positive defenders of the Bible, they are remaining silent because they are quietly doubting the authority and infallibility of the Holy Scriptures; if any of Christ's disciples have become troubled and dumb before the boastful skepticism of this nineteenth century,—let them take the deserved reproof of the Master: "If these shall hold their peace, the stones will cry out." The voices of the stones we have been hearing in the testimony of the monuments in Egypt and Assyria, in Babylonia and Palestine, and they have been as the voices of "many waters," breaking like the thunder of the multitudinous ocean upon this distant century at the "ends of the ages."

APPENDIX.

Note 1.—Page 24.

As bearing on the Canon, that ancient manual or summary of Christian truth, "The Teaching of the Twelve Apostles," discovered in manuscript in a library of Constantinople in 1875 and published in 1883, and assigned to the close of the first century or to the beginning of the second,—this venerable document shows familiarity with Matthew, Luke, and John in particular, and with apostolic doctrine in general. Then Papias, a contemporary of Justin, but older than he, in a passage preserved by Eusebius makes specific mention of the Gospels written by Matthew and Mark.

Note 2.—Page 33.

With regard to the Vatican Manuscript, it is a satisfaction to add that whatever embarrassing restrictions may have existed heretofore, scholars now are given generous access to the manuscript, Professor Schaff (as stated by him in a letter to the Rev. Dr. E. R. Craven) having recently been permitted to examine it for two days in the reading-room of the Vatican Library.

Note 3.—Page 37.

Of interest in connection with Aristotle's lost works was the announcement (January, 1891) of another great literary discovery. A collection of papyrus rolls from an Egyptian source having come into the possession of the British Museum, three of these were found to contain the larger portion of a long-lost and valuable treatise of Aristotle on the constitution of Athens, a knowledge of whose existence was retained only by some preserved fragments and by references to it in history. It is a Greek manuscript, assigned to the end of the first or the beginning of the second century. On the back of one of the rolls a farm-overseer had kept his accounts. In these times of archæological surprises it is almost useless to state what the oldest manuscripts are. Among recent discoveries are the Petrie papyri, which came from Kurob, in the Fayoum. These are Greek manuscripts, assigned to the third century before Christ at the latest, and which include portions of the Phædo of Plato.

Note 4.—Page 39.

A few chapters of the Old Testament were written in Chaldee.

Note 5.—Page 45.

Different editions of the Great Bible varied more or less, a continual revision going on. The Scripture of the Prayer-Book up to 1662 was taken from the fourth edition of this version, printed in 1540, with some slight emendations subsequently made, earlier and later. And when the Epistles and Gospels and

Sentences were made to conform to the Authorized Version of 1611, the Psalter and Canticles and the other biblical portions in general were retained in the phraseology of the Great Bible, which was felt to be more euphonious, and which also, particularly in the Psalms, had been learned by heart, and had thus become strongly intrenched in the affections of the people. (For this information the author is indebted to that excellent Episcopal authority, the Rev. Charles R. Hale, D. D., LL.D.)

Note 6.—Page 99.

The Nabonnedus Cylinder reads: "As for me, Nabonnedus, the king of Babylon, preserve me from sinning against thy great divinity, and grant me the gift of a life of long days; and plant in the heart of Bilusarra-utsur (Belshazzar), the eldest son, the offspring of my heart, reverence for thy great divinity, and never may he incline to sin; with fullness of life may he be satisfied." That prayer was not answered, but the clay document proves the existence of the needed person at the right time.

Note 7.—Page 106.

The identifications of the signets of Haggai and Jeremiah need not seem incredible, since an undoubted present possession is the well-authenticated signet-ring of Cheops, the builder of the Great Pyramid, who must have used that little ornament, that was also useful, in sealing orders given to the one hundred thousand men who, changed every three months, were forced to labor on the pyramidal mound for years, till the most prodigious architectural pile ever erected by man rose to the height of nearly five hundred feet and covered an area of about thirteen acres, long centuries before the two prophets were born.

Note 8.—Page 113.

Agassiz's well-known and pronounced opposition to materialistic evolution may make it seem improper to call him an evolutionist at all, and yet he may legitimately be classed with those who recognize a certain development in nature, while, after all, the supernatural is not entirely ruled out.

Note 9.—Page 156.

Babylon in her proud boast refers primarily to that Accadian "mount" of the "north" which was to the Oriental mind what the Olympian seat of the gods was to the Greeks, what Mont Blanc is to the Alps—the highest point of all. Babylon proposed to have a structure that would overtop everything, that would pierce the sky, that would rise above the very "clouds" and "stars."

Note 10.—Page 158.

An equally impressive lesson can be drawn if the mound of ruins going under the name of Babil be (as many claim) the true site of the ancient temple of Bel, for this also has literally "crumbled down."

www.ingramcontent.com/pod-product-compliance
Lightning Source LLC
Chambersburg PA
CBHW031353230426
43670CB00006B/530